SOME CALLED HIM
Bad Brad

The Autobiography of Douglas Bradley,
Nicknamed Bad Brad

Born June 17, 1963, to Present Day of June 17, 2022

Douglas Bradley

PAGE PUBLISHING
Conneaut Lake, PA

First originally published by Page Publishing 2024

ISBN 979-8-88793-603-1 (pbk)
ISBN 979-8-88793-619-2 (digital)

Printed in the United States of America

Sabrina Suzanne Bradley
January 30, 1986, to October 21, 1993
Samantha Dawn Bradley
November 01, 1990, to August 25, 2000
Passed away from complications of having a rare
spleen disorder called Niemann-Pick disease

CONTENTS

ACKNOWLEDGMENTS

Juanita Shelton for the love and support.

Steven Andreas for the long-term best friendship and deer-hunting.

Roger Eugene Bradley for being firm but fair.

Denny Keys, mentor and truck-driving instructor.

Shelly Bretty for loving and teaching me to ride a horse.

Judith Lorraine Bradley for being my mom and for the excellent closure.

Bryan Taylor for the loyalty and love.

Brent Taylor for being a loyal hunting partner.

Dawn Bradley for a sister's love.

Donna Bradley, the only woman that stood beside me.

INTRODUCTION

My name is Douglas Eugene Bradley, and I was born June 17, 1963, at Gulfway Hospital. Location: Gulf Freeway in Houston, Texas.

The hospital is no longer standing. I was a cute baby and a good boy; and four years later, my only sister, Dawn, was born at Saint Joseph's Hospital, Downtown Houston, Texas. I was special, being the first baby arriving, had blond hair and dark-blue eyes.

I had three grandmothers and one great-grandmother. Ma spent a lot of time with me and used to rock me high on her shoulder since I had asthma really bad. Later a miracle happened, and I just started breathing without any problems.

My dad was eighteen, and my mom was seventeen, in love (puppy), and we lived in Herne, Texas, by College Station. As a young boy, I remember only two things that stick out in my mind.

First thing: my dad was lighting a pit to barbeque with lighter fluid and put too much, catching our dog on fire.

My dad was controlling, jealous, and very young, so my parents fought a lot.

The second thing: I remember seeing my dad hitting my mom on more than one occasion. I've had a very interesting life, and I needed to write this book so I could vent and deal with some of my stress issues. I also thought about some other parents with sick children, and maybe they could be positive and overcome their heartbreak through my words regarding Niemann-Pick.

Life is full of ups and downs. And the only way you become strong is to become a survivor and believe in God.

I lost two of the prettiest angels that were godsent! I stumbled with depression but did not fall or give up on my two healthy children.

The good Lord will not put you through too much as long as you have faith in him. For any other family that has a very sick child, I'm very sorry. I can relate because I've been there. Niemann-Pick tore my family apart, and my wife blamed me first, then God. We tried to stay together, but the pain and guilt were too deep. We divorced in 1989, and Samantha Dawn and Sabrina Suzanne are buried in Land of Memory, located in Palestine, Texas.

My oldest daughter suffers from guilt and depression from the loss of her sisters. She could be bipolar like me. My son was a baby and only remembers his sisters a little. My ex-wife had a nervous breakdown, and depression is also a black cloud hanging over her life still today. I prayed for strength, and God helped me to be strong and positive for my two healthy children. Time has a way of healing a broken heart. We all had it rough back then, and my only regret as of 2014, there is still no cure for Niemann-Pick. I'd like to thank the Texas Children's Hospital in Houston for their professional staff and endless efforts. Dr. John Bellmont did not charge me a dime, and the care for my girls was A1. I'd like to thank Paul Herrington of Land of Memory Funeral Home, located in Palestine, Texas. He worked with me on paying out their burial plans. I had no insurance, and it was a miracle that he helped me.

I didn't blame anyone for this happening to me. My ex-wife cursed God and hit me one night when we lived on North Fowler Street. I used to pray to God and ask him to take me and spare them. He had his own plans for my girls. Some turn their backs on God; I'm glad I didn't. I had six years with one and nine with the other. I was thankful I got "the dance," where other parents lose their kids at birth. I can't, can't imagine.

My book is dedicated to my daughters, and I have and will continue to donate money to Make-A-Wish Foundation and Niemann-Pick Foundation. I will continue to pray for all these kids that have to experience some of these bad diseases out in the different states of the United States of America and other countries. If I can lend a helpful ear, please feel free to contact me at Mr. Douglas Bradley, cell number 936-438-9232 or 903-477-1522, anytime day or night. All chapters in my book are true. The names were left out for personal reasons. Writing this book was a challenge and helped me with my depression. I would have done anything possible to help the ending of the suffering my daughters went through.

C H A P T E R   1

The Bradleys

My grandmother was well off financially. Granny Bradley's husband must have rubbed off on her because she had rental properties, paid off houses, and money. My dad's mother, Juanita, wasn't good for my father. She would spoil him and then try to be firm on my dad.

One time in Spring, Texas, my dad asked to use the car on Friday night. She said yes, and he went out drinking at sixteen.

The next night, she said no. My dad cut all four tires with a switchblade. My dad finally straightened up around eighteen, and as a father to me, he was always very, very firm, but always fair. He got this from his dad, Tommy. The cycle continued because I got mine from them both, and this helped me in being a correctional officer.

I broke the cycle when I had my son, Shane Dakota Bradley. He is very shy and soft-spoken.

We have one family long tradition.

It is to flip the Y in Bradley.

This is something I've been proud of since I could write and goes back to my grandfather and World War II. My dad used to spank me hard with his belt, but my sister, Dawn, got away with murder and was the apple of his right eye. He would turn the other cheek, and I understood because she was his little girl. I give her hell and remember popping her and my cousin Rhonda with a bullwhip.

1

They told on me, and I got my butt torn up. Dad was a good father when he was sober, and he taught me at an early age on being a hard worker.

He would pay me to wash and wax his boat and vehicle. My sister loved Dad, and Dad loved us both but in different ways. My dad loved his boat, *Dawn 1*, fishing, and his beer. He worked as an auto-parts manager, and he was sharp. He could give you a part without looking it up, and he loved his job.

I used to work with him, and I was proud of him. I did not want to follow in his footsteps. I was his only son. I would get to see him one hour before school and some on the weekends. After work he would hit the beer joints every night and would stay there until 2:00 a.m. My dad's nickname was Jolly Roger.

Thomas Eugene Bradley picked out Dad's name from the B-52 bombers in World War II. They were called the Jolly Rogers. My dad was funny and always had a joke for you. His heart was big as Texas, but his downfall was the drinking.

My dad loved Galveston Bay and was a damn good fisherman. I remember my dad making me lie down on the floor of *Dawn 1*. He turned the boat in several dictions and said, "Boy, I just had a heart attack. Get me to the shore and call an ambulance." We were six miles out in the Gulf of Mexico.

I did it to get us back to the truck on the first try. My dad was so proud. I would always pay attention and listen to my dad.

Due to Dad's drinking, I quit going fishing with him. Every time he left to go, I wondered if I would see him alive again.

Ironically, in 2000 he left his mother's home in Palestine, Texas, for Louisiana. He wanted to try to get a tugboat job. Prior to this, his mother took my dad to John Sealy Hospital in Galveston. The doctor told my dad to quit drinking, or his liver was going to give out. When he left Palestine, I think he knew his days were few. He had a massive heart attack under the intercoastal bridge in Monroe, Louisiana.

In his left hand a beer, and a cigarette in his right. Someone took $800.00 from him when they found him on the hood of his car. How sad. A man who could have had it all ended up alone and with a beer. In 2000, before he left Palestine, he drove out to my house. He cried for me about the loss of my daughter and told me about the fight he had with Shelly, and he was headed for Monroe. We had closure. He said, "Boy, you turned out to be a hell of a man," and he wanted my number in case something happened to him. I gave him my address and telephone number, and he left. I cried and hoped he would be okay. I wanted to allow him to stay with me but could not tolerate the drinking. My dad didn't believe in doctors or the dentist. We said our goodbyes, and I wished him luck.

One week later, I got that bad call that my father had a heart attack. I was a mechanic for Walmart, and I will never forget dropping my wrench and running out of the shop after speaking to my boss, Eric, for the Walmart truck shop. I promised him I'd get him home, and we did. Mom, Dawn Shelly, Kurt, and I headed to Louisiana I kept my word and my dad a short fifty years on this great earth. Once identifying his body, I had to look twice to recognize Jolly Roger. He was in bad shape, and his body was a different color. The doctor told me his liver was in pieces. Dawn and I had Dad cremated and threw his remains in the gulf not far from Seabrook, Texas. I took after my dad more than my mom. Dawn is a lot like my mom.

I love to fish freshwater and saltwater a little. I saw how beer destroys a lot of lives, so I'm a mild drinker. I really loved my father, but as a young boy, I really wanted my parents together, and I told my dad once to quit drinking. Both of my parents didn't take care of their bodies. It was sad that they married young, divorced, and died young. My grandfather Thomas Eugene Bradley was a great man. He was a fighter pilot that flew B-52 bombers in World War II. I knew I get my strong backbone from him. He taught me a lot, and I skipped the eighth grade to make up for failing the first grade. His major was James Stewart, the movie star. He flew many missions and told me about the tracer bullets hitting the plane, but he never got a scratch.

He got out of the service and went to work for himself. I remember looking under his mattress and finding his military .45 auto pistol and stacks of hundred-dollar bills. He didn't believe in banks. Education was very important to Tommy. He gave respect and always got his respect back. I remember one night, during supper, my dad and him got into a physical fight. I was scared out of my mind. Tommy could have easily whipped my dad, but he didn't because I was there. My dad and grandfather were big men. My grandfather was a momma's boy though and was a very controlling man to his wife, Juanita. He had a tugboat and property off Navigation. He was a great businessman. One time I counted $10,000 under his mattress. He never lied and hated liars. I started to take a hundred dollars once to see if he would miss it, but I didn't. He hated a thief, and I didn't want him to lose respect for me.

In 1975 he was working under a truck on Navigation, and he was having problems with a bolt. He tried everything, even a hitting torch. He applied too much force, and the truck fell off the blocks, crushing his chest and killing him instantly. I was at the house with Granny Bradley when she got the call about Tommy's accident. Granny told me to ride my bike down to Navigation. Eyewitness 13 news channel was there. They put me on the news, and afterward I cried like a baby. I was scared, crushed, and so empty because my friend and hero was gone. We all took it hard. My dad and granny were quiet for months. Today I know I turned out to be the good guy because of his dedication to me. For months I would hear Granny at night crying in her bedroom. Granny loved us and loved her son. She was stressed, and she loved Tommy so much. Now that I'm older, I think of my deceased relatives, but then no one man can live forever; but when we lose them, we really miss them. One day I hope I get to see them again in heaven. Thanks for giving me a good start on this journey we call life.

CHAPTER 2

Childhood Memories

I really don't remember much about living with my parents. They married too young, and they were always unable to provide and fight. Their marriage lasted seven years. I was seven years old and my sister three years old when they went north and south. I remember Dad removing an engine spark plug or wires so the car wouldn't start. My mom always wanted to run back to her parents' home when they would fight. My dad loved the outdoors, and my mother hated it.

My mom was very sexy and beautiful. She shouldn't have married my father because my mother loved money and material things way too much. My dad smothered her a lot, controlled her, and to top it off, was very jealous. She wasn't allowed to wear shorts in public. How ridiculous. Caveman days are over. I was like that a little in my first wife's life, but I changed. I guess they both were immature, and I know fighting too much puts out any fire.

My mother's family grew up in a junkyard in Ohio. The Bowkers were uneducated, middle class to lower class, and came from a large family. There were four boys and four girls.

My grandfather, mom's dad, was a short, quiet man, and I remember a small image in my mind about him. My grandmother was a very devilish bitch of a mother toward all kids. She was a little less mean to Dawn and me. I remember as a very young boy and seeing her flip a couch over and place two of her grandkids down. If the kids would cry, she would stick dry-wash cloths in their mouths to stop the crying. My two uncles served time in TDC, the big house for petty crimes. My favorite uncle was in the KKK, Uncle Milton.

Mom was the oldest and felt obligated to take care of her sisters and brothers. And boy, she did that—gave them money and over-looked for them like one chicken looks after a bunch of baby ducks or chicks. Mom had to run off to find herself. Very sad story. She was too close to being negative about her job. When she left, she never called us or even sent us a birthday card. Her excuse: she had to find herself, become a millionaire, and she was afraid of our dad.

My great-grandmother was like a mother figure, but it wasn't the same. I can't express the empty feeling or guilt you have, not having both parents in your life. I remember looking for my mom's number once. I went through my dad's black book and found a Judy and called it, but it was my dad's old friend from Franklin, Texas. I was told by my dad to stop it.

Around ten years old, I really was missing my real mother and wanted her to find me. She was chasing her American dream of money and married for money and not love one time to my stepdad, Sonny. She was independent, and years later, I found out she was married to my stepfather, then drinking and control issues made her want to divorce and go back out, taking care of herself. She had her brothers laying carpet for her in the Pasadena, Texas, area and was bringing in clients and money. She even did Mickey Gilley's home.

In the end, before she passed away, we had closure. I forgave her for leaving and not being the best mother. She did the best she could. Mom, I did and still today (September 25, 2013) think of you daily, and I appreciate everything you did to give me my start.

Before her death from COPD and breathing problems and brain cancer, she had $130,000. After she paid off her bills, donated money to different Christian organizations, paid her boyfriend Jim, Dawn and I received ten thousand each. Dawn had filed for bank-ruptcy, and Mom gave her twelve thousand for that. I really didn't care, and to be honest, I was surprised she left me anything. Her sisters and brothers were upset their money train was gone. One of my uncles owed her thirty thousand, and still today I don't know if he paid her back.

She passed away on my birthday, June 17, 2008. I will never forget her lying in her bed. We moved her from Pasadena, Texas, to Friendswood, Texas. I, "Bad Brad," had to handle her brothers and sisters. The nurse came to me, telling me she was close to her passing. When Mom took that last, final breath, her two poodles ran to her window and barked. Her soul was good and free and gone. Dawn was crying and hugging her. I, Officer D. Bradley, proudly walked to the backyard and cried like a baby. I waited many years for her to be there for me, and after her life came full circle, it was time for her to go.

We had a beautiful funeral, and Brad Paisley's "I Know Where I'm Going" was her song. As I stood by her, Kenny Chesney's song was playing, and I cried pushing the button. She was my mentor. Mom told me life starts at fifty. She said, "I'm not worried about you, baby, but watch over Dawn and live life to the fullest." She never called me Officer Bradley. She did not like my nickname, Bad Brad. On Mother's Day, May 2012, I was depressed all day. I miss her a lot, and I'm hoping I get to see her again. Being with Miss Donna helped me that day, but I do miss her a lot. In the end, my mother asked me, her only son, to tell them all "she forgave them"

Her two brothers really hurt, hurt, and hurt her up to her death. In the summer of 2007, her two brothers were drinking and showed up at my mother's house. One held her down, and they had their way with her. Mother told me, and I pleaded for her to push rape charges on them, but she didn't. I as an officer first, son second, wanted to handle this. I turned the other cheek only for my mom's sake. Judgment day is coming, and the Bowkers will get everything they have coming. I got reports of some paranormal activity at their house after her death, and I know how powerful my mom was. Two days after her burial, my wife and I were driving up 45 North, toward Huntsville, Texas. My phone rang, and a scratchy woman's voice stated, "Baby, please help me cross over." It was an unlisted number. It scared me so much I dropped my cell phone, pulled over, and cried.

My mother never went to church, but she tried to get right with God and me. My mom had once a time a beautiful mind, body, and soul. She was a heavy smoker and really never took care of her mind or body.

Thanks, Mom, for your smile. For wanting me to be different than my dad. Being my coach about treating a lady like a lady and finding excellent closure with me and finally loving this little boy like I needed.

C H A P T E R   3

Living Off Wayside Drive

As a person, you never forget where you get your start. I believe life is a round circle: you have a start and you travel around the circle and you finally get to the end.

The year was 1972, and Eastend or Denver Harbor was basically an all-white neighborhood in the sixties, but the seventies brought a lot of Hispanics to Wayside Drive. It was so popular, with Prince's Drive-In and hot rods. Country singer, Waylon Jennings, wrote a song about Wayside Drive in Houston, Texas. How neat! My grandmother lived at 6832 Avenue I, behind Wayside and 69th Street since the fifties. My father had a roadster with a Hemi motor, and man, he said it was something else. On the weekends, for extra cash, he would bet other guys, if he placed a fifty-dollar bill on the dash, they could not catch it off the line. Roger won a lot of money. No one could catch that floating fifty-dollar bill.

My grandmother owned a small hamburger building. It was called Dairy Dream. I was twelve years old, and I worked there like my dad did. I started working four hours at night, and on my break, I would fix me up a great hamburger and fries and a large fountain drink. I enjoyed working there, but that was to become the last fast-food job I had. I got paid every Friday and was making a minimum wage of $5 an hour, plus an allowance for mowing my grandmother's

9

yard. Granny Bradley was teaching me the meaning of earning the American dollar.

I learned early, if I wanted anything extra, I could work for it. I liked money, so I mowed lawns for my neighbors and bought my first dirt bike from a friend off Canal Street.

Granny Bradley was a great provider, and I never had to worry about anything except getting jumped by gangbangers around the hood. All our bills got paid, and I never remember our lights going out unless there was a storm. Yes, Granny Bradley had money. She was a kind woman with a big heart. Made us go to church on Sundays, and I remember smelling fried chicken once, hitting the corner of Avenue I. Back then, churches had Christians that were pleasant to be around.

I accepted the Lord as my savior, got baptized, and went to church on Wednesdays and Sundays. Granny used to watch soap operas, and I used to sit in her old rockers, playing with her hand down, skin under her arms. She was old-school. When we would start to get sick, she would rub Vicks on our chests. It worked. I had one white friend, and Kenneth and I loved to play street football. I played baseball and remembered not listening to the coach about using my left hand to block the ball from coming up and hitting me.

One game this power hitter hit me the ball at shortstop, and the ball hit my left eye, causing a black eye for two weeks. After that, I listened to my coach. I was good at any sport I tried and later played basketball at our Baptist church. I practiced every day, but under stress, I was not very good at layups. I got good at free throws, and the hook was my favorite shot. Kenneth and I would spend nights together. He had a Honda 250, and I had a Honda CT70. Kenneth would always blow me off the street and the dirt. On Fridays we would watch Friday midnight special with Wolfman Jack. I hate to admit this to anyone, but I used to be a coward. I didn't want to fight. I was one of the few white guys that went to Edison Junior High. My dad caught onto me, walking out of my way from school, and he told me, "Boy, stand up and fight, or they will keep picking on you."

Well, I used to watch *Kung Fu* with David Carradine. I had the moves down. One afternoon the Spider Gang, five Hispanics on bikes, surrounded me. I got ready and kicked two of the boys, and the older ones left me alone. I wasn't Bad Brad until I was an adult, but it worked; they left me alone. Later, at Black Junior, I whopped up another bully that grabbed my steel jack stands. You fight enough, you start liking it. You get good. One afternoon Granny sent me to the store for milk. A badass gang member walked up to me and put a switchblade to my stomach for fighting and whopping his brother. I told him the truth, and it saved me a stabbing. I stated he jumped me first, and I was trying to get my respect. He let me make it. For years, I had nightmares about that long, black, dangerous blade. Now, my favorite stories about good old East End: girls, girls, Hispanic ones. I was pretty popular. Had several crushes on Josie, a beautiful cheerleader. She wouldn't give me a chance, but I dedicated a love ballad to her by Andy Gibbs, Bee Gees, brother. Sylvia Martinez was my first girl to kiss me at church. I saw stars and fire rockets. The Brady Bunch was popular, and I was happy as I could be. We would hold hands under her sweater because her brothers were so protective and really didn't want her to date me or any white guys. We finally broke up. She met some older guy with a car and went sex-crazy. Mary Ann was a taller, big-busted girl, and one weekend the girl really showed me her true colors. We went to Huntsville State Park for us to go swimming and hiking. After a long, private walk, she was a tease. It was over before it got started.

I had a Hispanic friend. We would sit on his porch, and he would tell me stories about his life. We talked even about sex. As a young boy, he grew up in Richmond, Texas, a farming community outside Houston. He said, once a week, his mom and dad would drive the buggy/horse to town for supplies. He had a garage apartment and rented it out to an illegal Hispanic that had two daughters from Mexico. He spoke to Mario, and she had always wanted a bicycle. Well, to make a long story short, she got the bike, and I got taken upstairs one weekend when her parents were gone. At thirteen, I became a man that felt eighteen.

That started my downhill crash with the opposite sex. My grandmother was old and started really having medical problems. My aunt would come out once a weekend to help pay her bills. My aunt and her husband started working on Granny Bradley's money. They were so caring and so fake. It worked. Granny put them over her will. Dad's drinking had gotten worse, and after some gun-pulling on my dad's part, CPS was called. Dad moved out, and we, Dawn and I, went to our aunt Shery's house to live. Dad moved to Anahuac, Texas, and stayed by himself. I, on the other hand, was surrounded by three girl cousins and my sister. It was weird going to an all-white school. Dad was in his own element in Anahuac, Texas. Working part-time auto parts, and finally, that ended. He was chasing his demons, and he woke up one morning in the middle of the highway. So his mother, Ma, had to drive down there to get him, and she took him to Palestine, Texas, to live with her. He stayed there and worked around the yard for her, and she was buying him a case of beer daily. He got a job at Auto Zone but was finally fired for having beer on the property in his truck. He got his income tax and finally came to grips his own way. He was dying, so he left for Louisiana. A doctor at John Sealy told my father, if he didn't quit drinking in six months, he would be dead. Roger Bradley told the doctor and everyone he didn't care. He was drinking himself to death. It was weird, saying goodbye to East End or Wayside. We the Bradleys lived there a long time.

Well, back to Aunt's house off T. C. Jester. I was adjusting going to Black Junior High. It was cool. All the girls were white, black, or Hispanic, and real pretty too. I tried out for basketball but didn't get picked. I wasn't popular until I got in high school years later.

Living with three girl cousins was strange but had its benefits. Yes, "girls." My cousins fought like cats and dogs. I met Steven, and we became thirty-eight-year-old friends. I was a normal white guy. We had fun until we hung around Floyd. He talked all of us into sneaking into the gym and stealing Waltrip jackets and shirts. I knew it was wrong but followed along. I thought if I got rid of the jackets, my crime would disappear. Wrong. It didn't work.

C H A P T E R   4

Moving to Northwest Houston

After admitting to my part of the crime, we all had to do community service. My best friend, Steve, and I let Floyd talk us to breaking into the school gym, and we stole shirts and shorts. I learned a valuable lesson: don't do the crime if you can't do the time. I had a dirt bike, and I couldn't ride for months. That really hurt. My crime days were over. Crime doesn't pay.

Granny Bradley was getting bad. Her mind was slipping, and at night I would lay in bed and hear her crying out for her mother. It broke my heart. One afternoon we all visited her in the hospital. The next day, after school, my aunt Sherry said she was gone. The grandmother I knew like a mother had left me. I was crushed, and life was going to be different now. She was one hell of a lady and a loving woman. We all missed her dearly, but my aunt and uncle Mike only cared about her money. I didn't. I wanted her back. They started spending her money, and I hated them for that. Two weeks later, my aunt sat Dawn and I down and said my mother wanted to see us. My mouth hit the floor. I hadn't seen my mother since I was seven years old. I guess it took money to get her to call her kids. We started seeing her on the weekends, and I couldn't stand my own mother. She was self-centered and a heavy smoker. She had different men around and was a gold digger. There was no respect and a lot of hatred on my part.

13

I was fifteen and very rebellious. I gave her a chance. Dawn was okay with her because she was too young to remember anything. My resentments and anger were causing problems. She told me I was going to respect her. I knew it had to be earned, and she hadn't earned it. School was out, and Sherry wanted us to go live with our mom. So we did. Sharpstown in Houston was our new home. She had a cleaning business and did carpet-cleaning. We would stay alone when she worked, and I loved that.

She was always down on me, but at first, she was nice. I couldn't understand how a really good mother of two healthy kids could just leave her kids to go off for years to find herself. No phone calls on birthdays, not even a card. Too me that is not love. All this affected me deeply. After a while, she started dating Sonny, her second husband, but they divorced. He was controlling and drank.

We met him at his home off Poinciana, and I liked him a lot. He was gentle and kind and had a lot of German in him and a funny sense of humor. He had two sides and style. He was like a gangster and a panda bear. After a while, Mom decided to remarry Sonny. She said it was for us. I think it was for her. He bought her a Lincoln and diamonds. What woman doesn't fall for that? She did love him, but she used him, and I did not like that. He was good to all of us. My mom used all men, and her love meter went off louder, depending on how much money they had. I did not believe this was right, and after seven years, they divorced, and Mother took him to the cleaners. At the hearing, I told her off, and she did not like the truth. I felt so sorry for him. I have always kept in touch and still call him dad. He taught me to hunt and supported me in sports.

Sonny had two grown sons, Mark and Sparky, and Chere in high school. My stepsister was so beautiful she could have entered pageants. We went waterskiing one weekend before they got married. She was supposed to go, but she couldn't make it. I was disappointed. We had a blast. My mom's brother, Billy, had speedboats.

With a jet boat, anyone can learn to ski. At first, I had a crush on Chere; but after they married, I realized she would always be my stepsister.

I liked her friends, and I was starting to get into girls, girls. I would see my stepbrothers on the weekends. Mark was the rebel, and Sparky played football, Sonny's favorite. He was good enough for the pros but had a knee injury. Christmases were great at the Kuehn's. We were a family, and I was growing up. I loved being a teenager.

I went to Scarborough High and was very cute. I was popular with the girls. I played baseball and football. Every weekend I would wash my mom's Lincoln and take out a different girl. Yes, I was a little stud, and my mom would call me a stud peacock. I was only getting to second base with the girls, but I was having fun. I got to play in the Astrodome twice; that was the bomb. High school was so cool. For many years, life was great. Mom was trying to be a mom, and she got me a clothes card, and I had it all because I worked at Kmart. When I got my driver's license, I had to parallel park my mom's Cadillac. I passed but knocked over a cone. That night I went cruising at the mall where everyone hung out. I should have been a pimp. I thought I died and went to heaven.

At work, I met Roxanne and had my first case of puppy love and got my heart broken for the first time. She was Hispanic, and her mom made her break up with me because I was white. I fell for her too fast and will never forget the night I picked her up. We were going to see Urban Cowboy. I asked her what was wrong, then I asked her if she wanted to break up. She said yes. I turned Sonny's half-ton around and drove her home. She didn't want to get out, then she said it was her mom's idea. I left, and I was crying, and she was too. I started going to the batting cages and dating several girls. Steven and I would go out on Saturday nights clubbing, but that stopped when Texas changed the drinking age from eighteen to twenty-one. I'd love to see Roxanne again. She was so pretty.

One Friday night, I was at the mall, cruising, and I saw a coworker parked in her new 5.0 Mustang. I pulled up to close, and my doorknob hit her car, scratching it. I was so embarrassed, and she didn't want to take a ride with me. She was mad as hell. She and I traded insurance information, and I told Mom late that night while she was asleep. Mom said, "Baby, don't worry about it. We will look at it tomorrow." What a relief. That was the only accident I had. We paid for Wendy's Mustang, and I never got a date. Too bad, too sad. She was older than me, and I could have made it to third base. Many years later, I took a defensive driving course.

Sonny and Mom bought a club in Pasadena and was drinking a lot. They were starting to fight a lot also. Their marriage was suffering, and Mom was taking this out on me. I was headed into the twelfth grade, and I started getting depressed. I had broken up with Debbie, and I called John, my second best friend in California. I asked him if could get away from my problems and get my head screwed on straight. He said yes, so I said my goodbyes and dropped out of school and ran away from my problems. This started a long history of unstable life I turned into and hated about myself.

C H A P T E R 5

Running Away to California

Well, John sent me $200 for a one-way ticket to Los Angeles, California. Before I left, I found out Karen, a close friend I was staying with, was in love with me. I broke her heart and told her I only loved her as a best friend. That bus drive was four days long, and we stopped in every town, so I had a lot of time to think. I wanted to get Douglas Bradley back on track, and I was blaming Mom for my problems, which was wrong.

We all have our problems. I arrived Downtown Los Angeles at 4:00 a.m. I stepped off the bus to observe the police chasing a man with a gun, and I was scared out of my mind. I finally saw my longtime friend, John Allen, and we headed for his truck several blocks away. He locked his keys inside, so he busted out the window, and we got out of Los Angeles. He lived in Chino one hour away. The mountains were beautiful, and it was totally different than *Texas*.

I had fun in California. I worked as a painter with John. We painted filling stations. It had been years since we saw each other, and we were best friends. John grew up in the oldest town in Texas, Nacogdoches, and got ran out of town for dating the sheriff's daughter and being Evel Knievel on a Honda street bike. So him and Grandma moved to Houston.

He was a supergood friend, and we met at my aunt's house on Bron Holly. We used to drive his blue Spitfire around the neighbor-

17

hood, looking for chicks. We could drive all on $3.00 on gas. Those were the days. Sueann was his hot cousin with great breasts, and all the boys wanted their turn with her. Her mom and dad were strict on her, but she always had a boyfriend. She would flirt with me, and I was waiting my turn like a kid waiting on Santa Claus. She was something else. Steven liked her too, but he nor I got very far but dreamed of being with her. I took her to the Galleria Mall and gave her a bracelet. She gave it back, but I did get a great French kiss. We decided just to be friends. They finally moved away to Lubbock, Texas, or maybe Midland, Texas. Steven told me she got married young and had two daughters.

To Sueann, I'm sorry for your loss, and I hope you and your husband overcame your great loss. My wife and I blamed each other. The stress from this was great. Well, back to John and I. He had changed a little since he left good old Houston. He had one bad habit—loved smoke—and I did it a little, him a lot. I stayed out there for four months. His dad and him were fighting a lot, and I was getting home sick. So my stay was about over. One afternoon, John brought out a mirror with two white lines on it. My mouth dropped, and I said, "No, I'm good." All my life, I had refused drugs, and I wasn't going to start now. I was a snuff dipper, and that is a bad habit, but I hated smoking of any kind. I don't understand how people can use drugs, and they think it helps, but only makes your problems worse. If I can lose two kids to a disease without turning to drugs or alcohol, others can deal with their own issues.

It was time to go home to Texas! Where the buffalo roam and the cowboys live. I called my grandmother in Palestine, and she sent me airfare to fly home. I flew into Tyler, Texas, forty-five minutes from her home, "The Holy City." John begged me to stay, but I said no. When I saw him with the white powder, it changed the way I looked at him. I knew I had to finish school, and military and law enforcement was calling. I said goodbye to California, and John had a gold wing motorcycle, and I had every fat girl wanting rides. They were too big to ride. I guess they need love too. I had to come home to get a skinny girl. LOL. LOL. Ha! Ha! A little joke, but true. The last report I got on John was, he moved to Dallas, Texas. Met a girl, got married, and had a little baby. Thanks, John, for being one of my dearest friends. And I'd love to see you again one day.

Call me at 936-438-9232/903-477-1522, and we will talk about the old days and times we shared. You helped me get my life straight, and I will never forget you until one day I die. We had fun, and I'm waiting for my cell phone to ring.

CHAPTER 6

Coming Home to Texas

The flight was great. My aunt Shelly picked me up in Tyler, "gave me a hug," and said, "Boy, are you crazy?" If only she knew the truth. See, I've always have been crazy, and it has kept me from going insane!

My grandmother called my mother, and for two hours, she laid the lowdown about the past, future, and me. What a great woman she is and has a solid back bone to support herself and our family. My mother was jealous of Ma and resented me/her in a lot of ways. No one told Judy Lorainne Bradley to leave. She did this and missed out on a lot of good memories. Soon Mom and Dawn came up to Palestine, and we started our rocky relationship. I went to summer school because my mother told me, "You'll never finish" Sorry, Mom, I did and received my high school diploma from Scarborough Senior High through Palestine High School. She called me and said "she was wrong and proud of me." My great-grandmother helped me get my second vehicle, a 1977 Ford Pinto station wagon. I went to work at TGY as a stocker, and one of my weekends off, I'd drive down to Pasadena, Texas, to visit Dawn and Mom. Mom had a new boy-friend, Ben, who was a welder and a superman. They were together for years, and I finally started to get to know Mom, and we had fun. Eventually, Ben passed away of a heart attack. Dawn and Mother were fighting, but Mom loved Ben. He drank, but not all the time.

Dawn was almost out of school, and they fought because they were alike in so many ways. I went to the funeral, and Mom divorced Sonny again. I tried to be loyal, but told my mother, how could she do this to my dad, Sonny? In my eyes, he was a real dad to me. I walked by my dad in the courtroom. He touched my shoulder. I said I loved him and would be around and would stay in touch. Still together I call him and "love him with all my heart." I made my mother cry that afternoon, and she got mad at me because at eighteen years old, I called her a gold digger! The truth hurts, but it has always set me free. She could have been fairer. My uncle got involved, called Sonny to keep him at the club, while my mother stripped the house and their bank account. They had $38,000. Mom left him a little. How shitty!

Even took the light bulbs out of the house. I saw how good and gentle this man was to her and us. Right is right, and wrong is wrong, and there isn't no in between. I felt so bad for Dad! After Ben's death, I got reports my mother tried to claim his house and take it from his real daughter. Luckily, the daughter fought my mom in court and got to keep her dad's home. They weren't legally married, and I never met Ben's daughter, but I'd like to say, "I'm sorry my mother, Judy, did this to you."

My mother could be a bitch! And the root of "all evil is money." My mother was ruthless and greedy when it came to money. The most money I've made all my life is thirty-two thousand a year. Through my mom's mistakes, I swore I'd treat people like I'd like to be treated, and money has never, will never, change my good character.

Well, on with the truth. Dawn and one of my cousins moved to Dallas. Shortly after that, I received a call from Ma in Palestine. My sister was on a dangerous road. I was stationed at Fort Hood, Texas, Killeen Copperas Cove area, so I told my wife I was driving to Dallas to speak with my sister about her decisions. I spoke to Dawn and Chris, and they came to Palestine. Before leaving, they took money and a pair of shoes from Ma without asking. With Mom, we could not get along. So I backed off. Dawn, my sister, lies every other word, so I tried to help her, but the redhead wouldn't listen, so I backed off from her too. Ma and I were close, and she was like my mom.

Between her and Granny Bradley, it was a tie for first place. Without these women, I would have turned out differently. I feel like Ma was born for herself and all her kids. She is a survivor and always gives great advice. Shelly resented our relationship. Sorry, I never put my hands on her like the fight y'all had in Florida. Read the Bible. It said to honor thy mother and father. I never hit my mother, and there were times I could have. One time she called me "a little boy" and said I was not an officer. I was so pissed I walked away and hit a two-by-four and broke it. I didn't talk to her for two and a half months over her using her mouth to harm me. Well, things have a way of working themselves out. This chapter had a lot of drama and negative things that I had to go through. I don't do drama and will handle anyone that gives it too me.

My sister straightened out but did something I don't care to write in my book. Our relationship has never been 100 percent. Mom and I saw it over every year, and I drove on like the Pony Express.

Steven and I became friends, deer-hunting buddies from November 6 of each year through January 3. My next chapter is a long favorite one of mine, about my boy adventures in Franklin, Texas. I have to take several writer's cramp breaks to get to the next chapters. Writing this book has been so rewarding for me. Living in Texas is a blast. In our state, we have oceans, deep East Texas, West Texas, and a lot of good people that make our state a diverse place to live in.

Thanks, relatives, for being dysfunctional and allowing me to remember all my stories to put on paper to share about my life.

C H A P T E R   7

Growing Up in Franklin County, Texas

This will be a long, very exciting, and boyhood chapter, covering living way back in the country.

After my parents divorced in the seventies, it was decided I would move to a small Texas town. I had my sister with me, and Ma was bored, and I think my dad wanted to work on getting my mom back, so he sent us to his mother's place. Franklin was small, the kind of town that everybody knew each other's business. Ma was renting an old, wooded two-story house built on top of an Indian cemetery. This house was so scary and old, and it was always making weird sounds. We lived there for five years, and during this time, we had some paranormal activities, mostly upstairs in the attic, guest bedrooms, mostly dead smells. Once we investigated the smells, they were gone. Shelly was in junior high, and I was in the first grade, and Dawn was a toddler. Shelly lived upstairs, and across the hallway was a corridor door that led into a large guest bedroom with a rock attic off to the left. It was scary-looking. I wasn't allowed in Shelly's room, her queen bee rule, and I didn't want to go anywhere in the guest room. It was haunted. Ma, Dawn, and I slept downstairs, and my grandfather worked with Union Pacific Railroad as a dispatcher and was only home on his days off—which weren't too many.

23

My aunt Hazel and her grown girls would come up from Baytown, Texas, and they wouldn't make it all night long sleeping in that room. Something would run them downstairs. You could hear voices coming from the attic. Once my grandmother and I went to get a box out of the attic and smelled the nastiest smell. We went back downstairs for a flashlight, came back, and the smell was gone.

Lights would flicker on and off, and once a light bulb exploded. It was like some spirit was always letting you know it was there. The television in that room would, out of the blue, turn on, or you'd be watching TV, and it wouldn't stay on. We had that TV checked, and no problems were ever found' it was a new black-and-white. Doors would creep open a little, and you always felt like someone was watching you. Real spooky! Attic doors would slam shut. Aunt Hazel was my grandmother's sexy sister, and several times she complained of something or someone touching her. She would always get woken up at the witch's hour of 3:00 a.m. from either the attic or the bedroom. You all get the picture. Once my grandmother sent me to get a box, and the door locked or got stuck. Those doors in the seventies mostly didn't have locks. I was freaking out, and my grandmother ran up there to save me, and that door was like someone was holding it from the other side. Yes, I believe in ghosts, Big Foot, and UFOs. I never went in that room again, but other than that, we loved our old house. One time Shelly was asleep in her room. It was late, and her back was to her door. That door opened slowly, and she felt something touch her. She woke up because the spirit told her to "get out." She did. She ran downstairs, yelling for her mother. The good memories were a birthday party, my eighth, I believe. Dad dropped fifty-one-dollar bills, and I had to follow, picking them up. I thought I was rich.

One Christmas I went to bed early and had the milk and cookies out. Woke to the thought it was morning time to open presents. I busted Shelly and Ma being Santa Clause. I didn't believe in Santa anymore. You should have seen their faces. I still love Christmases. The snow, lights, singing, and my first daughter, Sarah, was born in Germany. The nurses brought her to me in a Christmas stocking.

Well, it was time to move out to the hill. Our nearest neighbor was six miles away, and our rented house sat on a pretty big hill. We had so many outdoor memories there. One day we drove by our old house and saw it being bulldozed. We found out later it was built on top of a cemetery. That explained the unresting spirits.

In any state, you aren't supposed to disturb any graveyards. There is a new brick home there, and I never asked, but I'm sure they are experiencing some activity. Shelly was in high school now, and she loved horses. They bought me a one-eyed black pony called Midnight. We would ride a small school bus twelve miles to and from school. It was so cool. Shelly and I would go on long horseback rides. We would see deer and every kind of animal out there. Late one night, my great-grandmother almost hit a bobcat as long as the width of our '77 Ford pickup. It was so peaceful there. The Fultons had a lot of cows on the property. Ma and Shelly bought me my first jet-black Shetland pony. We named him Midnight. Midnight was a great horse. He had one problem. His previous adult owner, we'll call him Mr. Dick Smith, was a beer drinker. One evening he didn't have any luck catching Midnight, so he made a very bad decision. He probably was mean to the pony, and this smart pony kept running from him. It went on and on. Finally, Mr. Dick Smith went to his truck, grabbed his 30-06 deer rifle, shot once at Midnight, grazing his right eye. This pony was lucky. When Shelly and I would go exploring, we would ride for hours, or days. We had a blast. Trail rides were popular in the seventies. And we one have story that really sticks out like a sore thumb. Back in the day, my grandmother was a little bit of a beer drinker. We had finished riding for the day. Wagons were unhooked, and the big pot of beans were cooking, and almost everyone in camp was drunk. My grandmother farted so, so loud, and some drunk cowboy yelled out, "Hold it down. It's pumping mud." We all laughed out loud. Even the crickets quit chirping.

Shelly, my loving aunt, taught me to ride at an early age. We jumped creeks, swam in lakes, and explored the woods. Found a young fawn tried to make her a pet. It worked, and when we all moved to Palestine, a German shepherd barked, and Shelly's pet deer ran off and got its freedom. Midnight was a jumper. We would put up cane poles ten feet high, and I would clear it 95 percent of the time.

My first gun was a BB gun. I was told not to shoot out the night-light. What did I do! When Ma turned her back, "shoot 'em up." I busted the glass and got a spanking. Every winter, a thousand black birds would fly in and land in these large oak trees. I had a field day. I wanted to deer hunt but was too little. My aunt Hazel's husband came up from Baytown, and I showed him where a big buck was crossing the road. Sunday morning 7:00 a.m. I was in bed and heard his rifle sound off. He paid me $50.00, and he got that deer. My first girlfriend was Shirley Gale. We would sleep under the stairs on lawn chairs, and I told her one day we were going to get married one day. She moved away, and I never saw her again. In the summers, we would go swimming in stock tanks, and I would get so sunburned I almost got skin cancer. I never used sunscreen even though Ma told me to use it. I was so hardheaded.

C H A P T E R   8

Saying Goodbye to Franklin, Texas

I was in the second grade, and I failed it twice due to not doing the work, and I moved back and forth from Houston and Franklin. Ma drank a lot, and most of the time, Shelley watched me. Ma spoiled me and had a verbal fight with my teacher—another good reason I failed. I supposed Ma didn't whop up on her. Shelly and Karen were spending the night one weekend. Shelly came home and told Ma what the girls' mom said about Ma. Ma called her and threatened to whop her. The lady called the sheriff's office. Deputies came out to the hill and fought Ma and arrested her. They left me in the house with the fireplace going. My grandmother has Indian blood and grew up in Oklahoma. You don't mess with Charlene Shelton. She is a fighter. She called in the *Texas Rangers*, and they investigated the sheriff. He did not get reelected. It was a big stink, but you don't mess with her, money, or her kids. She was the best until God called her home October 18, 2013, at the nursing home in Palestine at 9:13 a.m. I was the last one to arrive, and I feel like she waited for me. I said, "Ma, it is me, Douglas Bradley. Don't fight it. Go to the light, and Sam and Sabrina are waiting for you." One tear came down her cheek, and she was gone. I had lost the only mom and grandmother I knew. She was the greatest! I remember so many things about her and the hill. I remember my dad catching me in quarrel with a wild station. He had me grab his front bumper of his El Camino. I turned around and said, "Dad, are you through yet!" He saved my life that day. I was eight years old. He was mad because I laughed about his spanking. I respected my dad because he was so firm. He wasn't shy with his belt. Thanks, Dad!

My dad was a lot of fun. He would put us all on a hood of a car and pull us on the sandy roads with his El Camino. One time I fell off, and the hood ran over me. It hurt, but being hardheaded saved me. During hunting season, a Houston boy wandered off from deer camp and became lost. Shelly and I saddled up and searched all night. He was by the road, hiding in the bushes. He finally came out, and he was scared to death. Out there, there were wolves, coyotes, bobcats. That was a good feeling when we found him. His guardian angel was there that night.

Shelly and I went home and went to bed. We were so tired! One time my dad stopped by an old, abandoned house to pee. He heard a growl over under the porch. There was a lone female timber wolf. My dad fed her and made friends with her and after weeks brought her home to the hill, but when it would thunder, she would run back to the porch. They are creatures of habit. It was two miles back to that old house. That's neat and a true story. A few years later, some hunters shot her, and my dad was crushed. Another weekend Shelly and Karen got bored and decided to rope my pony, Midnight. The rope caught a bush and broke his legs. I was so crushed. I loved that horse, and he and I were best friends. Another weekend we were going to a wedding, and on a hairpin curve, we met my dad, driving fast and drunk, and had a head-on collision. We used to honk, but that day it did not work. Shelly broke her nose, Karen a black eye, and me twelve stiches in my knee. Virginia had no injuries had to walk back five miles to get Ma. Dawn broke her right leg in two places. Dad cut his leg bad. Ma brought the green '71 Ford PU and took us to Hearne to the hospital. Dad walked to his camper and would have bled to death if it wouldn't have been for two state troopers coming out. Thanks, troopers. Knock one up for the good guys! My dad had guardian angels. My dad had two bad wrecks and two DWIs. What are the odds of your own father hitting you? Back then, they popped you on the wrist; today you go to TDC. I say, don't drink and drive.

My dad's grandmother, Hazel, did some crazy things. Poaching was for meat for us to eat, and back then, you never heard of a game warden, maybe one for twenty counties. They would drive over to a small town and shoot out streetlights. What a thing to do as adults. I learned how to swim by playing *king* of the mountain at a large lake with an island. I got threw in and sunk like a rock. My brain said, "Kick off," and I swam. I was through! My grandmother started to jump in, but my dad said, "Wait." We had a lot of good dangerous times. Ma's mother would come get Dawn and I and take us to her home in Marlin, Texas.

One weekend we went to Marlin with *Mema*, and across the street, there was a little bush full of red-hot peppers. She said, "Stay away." What did I do? Went over and got a mouthful. I started screaming. She came running over, scared half to death, and no lie, my mouth was on fire. Several hours later, the heat was gone. Still today I won't even eat pepper on my food. It ruined me for life. Mema was the black sheep of the family. She talked badly about everyone and followed Ma around like a lost puppy. She adored us kids, and when they would fight, she would come park and just try to see us. Back then, they didn't call it stalking. She passed away in a nursing home in Palestine, without a funeral. Ma had her ashes put in the ground by an oak tree. Hazel wouldn't even pay toward her own mother's death. Ma and Hazel were sisters, but different like night and day. In 2000 I drove back to Franklin. The house on the hill hadn't changed. A deer camp. The Fultons were gone, and the son Kevin inherited the cows and land. On May 23, 2014, Donna and I went, and I spoke to Kevin. Dawn and I went to Houston, and Ma and Shelly moved to Palestine. Years later, after his retirement, James Shelton passed away of cancer in Palestine. Shelly is on her second marriage to *Kurt*, and I love her even though she has always resented me. I will never forget Franklin nor Palestine. My childhood was fun. I'd like to thank Ma for being there always.

CHAPTER 9

Getting Married Way Too Young

The year was March 8, 1987, when I got married way too young to my first wife. She was seventeen. I was eighteen. We dated a short time, and I went to work for the highway department after going to school half the day. I finished high school and met at TGY. She was stacking alcohol, and I was sweeping, and she smiled at me. We continued to date, but her parents were very different and from Missouri (the show-me state).

One Friday I attempted to go bowling with, her but we were fighting. I think she didn't want to go. She was being a super bitch. I went to turn my Ford Pinto around, got to her driveway, and I told her to get out of the car. Before I knew it, she slapped me so hard it made me hit my head on the driver's window. She wouldn't get out of the car. I had to threaten to call Ma, and it worked. The next week, I broke up with her. I followed my heart, and it will never do you wrong. Her family didn't fall far from the tree trunk. She was just as back wooded as them, but I did not realize it. They lived in a single, dirty, small trailer with holes in the floor, and she had one older brother that drank like a fish. After a while, she called me and told me she was going to tell her dad I forced myself on her for sex. I was furious, and I told my grandmother. That was the start of a seventeen-long rocky, emotional, and physical relationship we had.

Ma called her and told her she better cool it. She always played dirty pool with me, especially with the kids.

One month later, I was at Dewayne's house in Long Lake, and I left to be pulled over by her dad flashing his lights at me. He told me she was unhappy and wanted us to talk. I wish still today I would have kept driving. I pulled over—big, big, big mistake. We talked and got back together. Grandmothers know best. Ma told me, "The apple don't fall from the tree." I wish I would have listened. I should have never married her, along with some of my ex-wives. But God has a plan for us all, and I never would have had my son or daughters, *Sam, Sarah, and Sabrina*. When you take a girl's virginity, they never forget you. Things were better, but in her parents' eyes, I wasn't good enough for her. Hell, I think it was the other way around. My fiancé was looking a way to get away from her controlling dad, and she hinted about us getting married. It's true. A rich girl wants to flirt, and a poor girl wants to marry.

I went down and joined the US Army, hoping to be an MP. My scores were too low, so it was between a cook or a mechanic. I chose mechanic. I was a solder first, and I loved serving my country and helped me to turn from a boy into a man. I only saw peacetime and got out right before Desert Storm started. She was in the twelfth grade, and she eventually moved in with Ma. The day finally came when I had to depart for Dallas, Texas. I will never forget the bus pulling away from her and Ma. It felt like my heart was on a chain. I admit, it was good for me to join. We had a lot of growing up. I was a little scared boy in a nineteen-year-old body. She was my second love, but we had a deep love for each other. Joining the military was so good for me. I took that oath, and next was on a 747 for Fort Jackson Columbia, South Carolina. I arrived at 4:00 a.m., went in, and got two hours of sleep. At 6:00 a.m. I got woken up by a bugle going off. I thought, *What have I got myself into? It is a different world from civilian life.* It was different and good for me. They teach you about pride, and so much more. A trade was what I was after. I completed *basic training*, a boyhood dream of mine. A lot of fun being yelled at and doing one thousand push-ups every day. I was in the best shape ever. I weighed 120 soaked and wet. I could do those push-ups.

Ma and my fiancé arrived for my graduation. I had one week to drive home to get married. We did the deed in a small church. It was May 14, 1983. We had about twenty guests, me in my uniform and her in a long white dress. We missed each other so much after being apart from March until May. We wrote a lot of letters, and she kept me going. Once I thought about dropping out. I was homesick, and the training was hard. We made it home in twenty hours. I was driving, and it was funny to see Ma pee in a bucket off the back seat of her car. She was drinking beer, and I couldn't stop every two miles.

On our wedding day, my new bride was so nervous her bouquet of flowers was shaking. We couldn't afford a honeymoon, so we went out to eat and stayed in the room for one and a half days. We both saved money. I had money, but when she arrived in South Carolina, guess what? She dropped her wallet with $800 in it. She got her wallet back, but no money. I told her to get traveler's checks, but she never listens. Two days later, my in-laws drove me to Dallas, and I was headed back to Fort Jackson mechanics school for seventeen weeks. My training was interesting, and before going in, I wasn't mechanically inclined. I had pride being a soldier, but I failed airborne. Only two things fall out of the sky, bird crap and airplanes, and I'm scared of anything over two stories high. After that, I went home for two weeks, went deer-hunting, and then I was starting my marriage and my career. We were young, immature, but at that age, you know it all, especially about love.

I caught another long plane ride for Schwäbisch Gmünd, West Germany. I hated to leave my wife, but I did it. I was going to find an apartment and would send for her after I got settled. She was so young, naive, but at first, she really loved me a lot. I loved her a lot but had no idea what was in store for me. Germany was different, and I was homesick, bad. I found an apartment four blocks from my unit. I rented it, sent her money, and SP-4 Joe Mast from Montana drove me to Frankfurt to pick her up. That night I didn't get much rest, and we got so drunk off German wine. I had to go to the field a lot, so she was lonely a lot. She made friends with a neighbor girl from Georgia, and that helped. We started talking about a family. And finally, she got pregnant. After my first daughter was born on

Christmas Day 1984, she told me she really wasn't ready to have kids. I was shocked and pissed. I wanted kids because I love them and they are sent from God. Her parents came over, and her mother was walking on eggshells and disrespecting me. The old man was trying to control me. We had a fight, and they went home. Our second fight, wife lied about a large telephone bill. She stayed on the phone to her parents while I was at work. I was highly upset that I had to pay five hundred to a German phone company because my wife couldn't keep from riding the fence post with her parents. She was lazy, and I begged her to get a job on base, but she had no goals for herself.

Sarah finally came out on December 25, 1984, and instead of being home, dreaming of what Santa brought me, I was holding a Christmas angel in a red-and-white stocking. It was so strange not waking up to Christmas but being in the hospital. She was cute, and we all made it home. It was snowing and beautiful, like my number one daughter. I was excited about my young new life and especially about being a dad. At first, I wanted a boy, but I came to accept Sarah was a girl. I wanted her to be a tomboy. One night we bonded. She was crying, and I was so tired. Her mother would not get up, so I did. I tried everything; she just kept crying and crying. I lost my patience and shook her, telling her to stop crying. I guess she wanted mom but was stuck with dad. She stopped, and for the first time in my life, I realized God had given me a beautiful, healthy baby girl. We rocked together for a long time, and both of us fell asleep in that rocking chair. That is the strongest emotion in the universe—*love*.

My grandmother came over to visit. I took leave, and the four of us traveled to Switzerland. The people were so rude. On the bus, I passed gas or farted out loud and blamed my wife in front of two soldiers. Bless her heart, she was so embarrassed. My grandmother knew what I had done. She just laughed and said, "Douglas." Ma left, and after that, I made the biggest mistake of my life and carried this great lie for a long time. I started neglecting my wife. Dave and I started going to a western club (Longhorn) in Stuttgart. I got so tired of everything. I didn't care, and my attitude showed everything. Height of the ceiling, I was ready to go home. My wife and I were fighting, and I didn't feel close to her or the baby. The guard duty was killing me every other night. I was looking for something different. Found it in the arms of another woman named Elka. Didn't sleep with her, but it was like I did. So I hurt my family and almost lost my wife and daughter to a dumb mistake on my part. My wife never forgave me and later on added more to the story to turn my daughter into believing her story. I told her the truth, and she almost went back to the United States. She was so, so, so hurt. I hated myself for kissing and touching an innocent German girl. She never forgave me, and I think she was scorned and vowed to kill me. She even paid me back twice later on—once in Houston, Texas, and once in Palestine. She took Sarah and went home early. I was crushed. Then I received orders for Fort Hood located in Killeen, Texas. Man, that was cool. We didn't get a divorce, so I rented us a trailer from Ray in Copperas Cove, Texas. Ray Chapman was a good man, a public servant police officer for Lampasas police department. I need to go see old Ray. Well, we had bad news. This is where our lives turned dark with depression, and we blamed it on each other about our sick daughters. I wish I didn't have to remember this, but I do.

Sarah was two, and every fight we had ended back on Elka in Germany. In her mind, we slept together, and I swear we didn't. If she would have forgiven me, we might have stayed married for us and the kids. On the weekends, we would drive home and visit. We noticed Sarah was doing most of the talking for Sabrina. We ignored it. My wife lied about her birth control pills, and Sabrina was falling down a lot. I missed school in the Army to help my wife, and I got an Article 15, lost a stripe and money. She and I decided, I was going or completing my four-year commitment, then I was getting out. She still lied a lot, and we took my daughter to a doctor in Palestine. Then doctors said she needed tubes in her ears. She was born with yellow jaundice read bad. I felt something was wrong, and I was right. We bought a mobile home beside Ma and took her to Tyler for testing for rare diseases. They thought she was a carrier of cerebral palsy, another disease.

I said goodbye to the army, and I'll close. Glad I turned into a man, but when they wrote me up over missing school, that did it.

Well, it was 1987, and we got our trailer in place, and I had applied for the *Texas Department of Corrections*. I had no regrets about the military and had an honorable discharge. I think every young man should go in for a two-year stretch. I'm sorry I had that weak moment in the back of that Volkswagen. Even as a husband, father, and soldier, I made mistakes. No one is perfect, especially me. You can read a book for picking your child's names, but there is no book on being a perfect father or husband. We had *Sabrina* tested and had to drive down to Houston to the *Texas Children's Hospital. We* all gave skin samples and were called back at a later time. We walked in, and Dr. Belmont said, "I have bad news. Y'all might want to sit down." I said I would rather stand. He said, "Your daughter has a rare spleen disorder called *Niemann-Pick disease* with no cure." I felt like he shot me with a gun. They had three types. It is like AIDS virus in a way. It breaks down everything—the walking, talking, motor skills—and they usually pass away quickly of an infection. We were shocked and heartbroken, and guilt took over our lives so quickly. Then depression took over. I fought it and continued to work my job at the Coffield Unit. I had to support my family even though I was depressed. My wife and I blamed each other, and Sarah took it hard. I wasn't mad at God, but I did not understand. Many, many times I said, "Why, God? Why us?" God never puts you through anything you can't handle. I became a stronger person and concentrated on the time we had. God is good! God is great!

C H A P T E R   1 0

Texas Department of Corrections

This is another long chapter and to me the most exciting. All my stories are true, and there is a lot of them. Here we go into one of the oldest prisons in the history throughout Texas!

The year was 1987, and I had just gotten out of the Army. I took the civil exam to be a *Palestine police officer* but failed the test by five points. So I applied for TDC. I had to go to *Gatesville, Texas*, for their academy. I wanted to go to work for them, and I made a fine correctional officer. One day, we were watching films on *Coffield*, where they keep the real badasses. They call it the end of the line. These guys love to assault the officers. I did not know at the time this was going to be my unit. I passed the academy, was twenty-three years old, and weighed 135, fit and trim. I thought I was ready for Coffield, my home away from home for the next five years. I will never forget walking in and those steel bars slamming between me and the free world. I was scared. We had one employee start crying and quit that day. It is not a job for everyone.

I had a week off then reported to the unit on a Monday. A lot of the inmates were staring at me. They said, "He blue eyes. We are going to pull you in our cells and rape you." I realized right away I was in a violent and different world. I was at the devil's playground, and it was my job to control security and correct these men when did wrong. In the academy, they taught us to be firm but fair and to always keep your word, so I did. They have so much time and nothing to lose.

One day, I was taking the black *inmates* out for their one hour of recreation I put the cuffs on and double-locked them. An average inmate started jerking and twisting around on me. He was calling me white pecker wood. I warned him twice to stop, and he got angrier. I said, "One more time. You are going on the floor." He said, "You ain't going to do anything." He was laughing at me, and my 135 structure. In there you have to have bulging muscles, and you are not feared. He hit me in the side, and we took off like a rocket for the bars. I hit his head on the bars, and he hit the floor like a ton of bricks. I grabbed a finger, twisting it, and it was so quiet you could hear a pin drop. He yelled out, "*Bad Brad*, you're killing me." That's how I got my nickname. At 2:00 p.m. I went home with my first use of *force* under my belt. From 1987 to 1991, I had a dangerous job and serious, responsible job. I loved my job. Every morning, I would jump out of bed and couldn't wait to get the day started. I started out on second shift, 2:00 to 10:00 p.m. A lot of showering goes on. I put in for days 6:00 a.m. to 2:00 p.m., and this was the shift I fell in love with. All the rank was there, but I didn't care.

I was a professional, and I was doing my job, and only the officers doing wrong have to worry about the rank. All the turn-keys got replaced. They used to run the prison. Now the officers do everything. The *Ruiz versus State* changed the prison and gave the inmates a lot of rights. A *state judge* was watching TDC closely. The next day, all the inmates were calling me Bad Brad instead of Officer Bradley. I was impressed. I had some respect, and I loved it. All the inmates were talking about me. If you are weak, they pick up on that real fast. If you are strong, others won't mess with you. I wasn't a coward anymore, and I loved the power I had, but never abused it. The inmates called us boss. These inmates have created a system that works well for them, and *state* is lamb to it. The strong feeds off the weak. Respect is earned by showing force every day. We had fights every day and stabbings when there was a hit put out on another one's life. When I hear "fight," I'd run, trying to be the first one there and the last to leave. I stood alone and fought alone. I backed up my fellow officers, and they had my back.

Another close call when I had (*Bad Brad*) stepped in was when Rex was going to court to get more time at the Palestine courthouse. He was going to get a life sentence. Captain picked me because he knew I would stay alert. We searched him and found nothing and headed off P2 ad seg unit. In the van, I was driving, and I noticed he was moving a lot. The officer in the back was catnapping. A big *no-no*. Captain was to my right, doing paperwork. We got to the courthouse, checked the cuffs, and proceeded inside. Walking up the stairs, *Rex* kept turning around. I told him to stop it. His mind was telling him to grab my 357 and try to escape. At the top of the stairs, he said, "Bad Brad, I need to go to the restroom." So I told the *captain*. He tried to close the door, and I blocked it. I unhooked my strap on my 357. I didn't trust him. He had one cuff off. I said, "Captain, get over here." I looked down at my belt to see if my key was missing. It was there. Captain said, "How did you get that cuff off?" In his teeth, he had a key. The captain took the key and said, "What were you going to do?" He said he was going to kill us and run. That was scary. Captain asked him what stopped him. He said, "I knew Bad Brad would have shot me dead." He was right I would have saved the taxpayers thousands. I spent hours on the block, and he was from Houston and crazy as a loon.

He got his life sentence, and we headed back for the unit. I went home that evening and kissed my wife and kids, glad I didn't have to kill him.

My goal every day was to go home with the same amount of blood I went to work with. At home, I was changing. A lot of officers treat their families like inmates, and this is so wrong. That is why the divorce rate is so, so high. The job is so stressful a lot of officers die in their fifties.

My job was negative, and I was taking my anger home to my family. I was controlling my wife band was way too hard on *Sarah*. The year was 1989, and over the holidays, we had major riots with a lot of killings. The worst one was the *Halloween* massacre. The Mexican Mafia and the blacks snuck weapons in the dayroom and went to town. The Mexicans won. It was over drug control. I was off but looked at the films—a bloody mess. There were lungs and hearts hanging off the bars. We let them get through, then we would shoot the gas on them and have them lay down. Back in the day, most officers were honest, and we were a team. Today it is a joke with all the bad staff. I worked there twelve years and never broke the rules or got written up. It's sad a great job changed to a day-care center. That's why I didn't stay twenty years. I was honest all the time.

The next riot I was involved in it happened on the PL rec yard. I was working 2:00 to 10:00. Around dark, they started fighting, then out came the knives. I heard, "Fight," and I took off, running for the rec door. I saw blood everywhere, told the boss to open the door, and he said, "Wait, Bad Brad, for other officers." So I did. We opened the door, and I started yelling, "Lay down." I said it three times. They wouldn't stop! I had my riot baton and hit this one Mexican so hard I broke his collarbone. When this happens, it is like your front end falling out from your car. He stopped fighting and dropped the shank. When it was over, one offender said my eyes turned from blue to red. The whites were in a group, staying out of it. They were scared, and so was I. There were body parts everywhere. It finally was over as soon as it started. Those were the days we called rock and roll.

My hero is real, and I was thankful I had to be Bad Brad at times. I used to be so weak and a coward when I lived off Wayside. I don't like to fight, but sometimes it is necessary. Through my blue eyes, I saw so many negative things at Coffield and other units I worked in. I remember the time a female officer was having problems at home and started meeting up with an inmate in the closet for sex. She then realized she was doing wrong with him and tried to end it. One day, she was working a crash gate, and he walked up to her and stabbed her twelve times and said, "If I can't have you, no one can." That is how they think. I got hurt one time in twelve years; I was lucky. The only thing that is positive was paydays, and some *inmates* find the Lord and try to make parole. Payday was one time a month; that was a long month. TDC is the fifth lowest paid prison in the *United States of America*. And they wonder why everyone quits.

After four years, I topped out as a coll, making 1,895.00 and bringing home 1,594.00. Today they are making a little more, but the *state* will give you a hundred and take back ninety-nine. Then they made it mandatory for overtime. Some bosses were working so much they were going out and paying cash for $5,000 four-wheelers. Then they stopped that. If the *state* would quit changing, things would be better. *California* is the best paying system. Well, back to my career. *Captain Hubert* was going to population from ad seg, and he asked me to go, said he would help me make sergeant. I said no. I wanted to be where the action was at. A lot of officers were beating up on the inmates. We called it clicking. I didn't do this, but I knew several that did, but kept clear of that. Inter affair was just waiting to fire some of these officers. Spaced mine out, and only did it when it was very necessary.

My great lieutenant finally got fired. He was a Hispanic, and he hated black inmates. The world we live in is so racial. I hated to see him go, but he stepped over the line. I heard he moved to *Austin* and went to work on boats. Well, my other white lieutenant was one hell of a supervisor. He was old-school too. One weekend, I had gotten drown for a deer hunt, and I asked him if I could get off a little early. He said, "Hell no."

I wasn't his favorite boss and wasn't in his clique. I went to *Sergeant Morton* and complained. He went to bat for me. At 1:00 p.m. the lieutenant told me to go get an offender out, and if he acted up, to slam him and draw blood. This was a test for me, and he was upset at the offender in which I knew nothing about. I warned him, and *Taylor* had the camera down on purpose. He tried to kick Taylor—big, big mistake. I picked him up, and he got about ten stiches that day. The lieutenant came up, touched my shoulder, and said to me, "Get out of here." I was shocked! "I've got this." I said, "What about my paperwork?" He said, "Do it in the morning." I said, "Thanks, lieutenant," and I hurried for the woods. Lieutenant was the best, and I respected the hell out him. *Huntsville* finally ran him and his wife off. The offenders were getting away with murder, and the soft officers were growing at an alarming rate. TDC was changing. I had not changed and wasn't going to. I was staying in the middle.

One *Sunday* I was going to *church* and had to stop for gas and a can of dip. I tried to open the door, and it was stuck. I didn't know Lieutenant Chastin was holding the door, messing with me. He said, "Boy, where you going?" I said, "Church." He said, "Why?" I said, "To keep the devil away." He said, "Hell, he will run from you, Bad Brad." That was funny, but the truth. He was my mentor. We shook hands, and I will never forget him.

Over the years, I got the reputation for being crazy. See, I had to be to survive. I like my nickname, and today I only see old Bad Brad every now and then. Well, back at work, I busted *Ricky Smith*, a young cop killer, shooting them in the back, trying to plan an escape. He didn't like I spoiled his plans. The next day, he jerked the cuffs, and I wired him up, and he was pulling on the cuffs. I let go, and he hit his back on the toilet. He said, "I'm going to get you, Officer Bradley." I said, "I'm here three hundred days a year. Bring it on, you coward." Well, several weeks later, he got me good, threw a piece of metal, striking me in the head. I wanted to open that cell, but I knew I would get fired. I think my boys gave him an attitude adjustment. I headed for the hospital. It took seven stitches in my head, and I believe that injury was the reason later I started having chemical imbalance. And then finding out I was bipolar. I wasn't the same after that injury. I tried to get back to the old Bad Brad. I was having problems. I had to go on *workers' comp*. I couldn't sleep, have sex, run like I used to. They offered me $3,000.00 for my injury. I said no. I didn't want to have an injury on my back. I still wanted to be a police officer. I got $5,000.00 on my injury. I resigned and moved to Houston and wanted to go to the *University of Houston* security course. One officer fell in a chair that broke and got $25,000.00 No one would hire him again. I loved outside security.

My father-in-law didn't like I took his daughter to Houston, but I had to do it for me. I got a patrol security job at *Metropolitan Security*. They had ten thousand acres, including a mall off *Gessner*. Hell, I was like a police officer, and I loved being outside. Money was fair and less stressful. You have a place to back up in TDC. You can't escape the danger. I missed the prison but was dealing with it. In time, my injury got better. For three years, I was a patrolman. I worked with HPD and *Harris County*. I felt like a peace officer. I only had to be security, and I was protecting and —— an assault at the Olive Garden. I took the report, got a good description of the suspect, and was driving, looking for him. I put it out on the radio, and I saw him at the bus stop. *He* was a tall black male. I pulled up and got out of the car and told him to get on the hood and spread his legs in which he did. He said, "Okay, boss," and I knew he was one of my TDC boys. He said, "Bad Brad, don't shoot me." I was surprised he knew me. It's a small world out there, and you never know who you will bump in too. I drove him back to the Olive Garden, and I told him to shoot straight with me, and I could help but lie, "You're going to jail." The older couple identified him as the suspect that hit the man in the face because he would not give up a quarter. Yes, a quarter. I searched his wallet, and he had $120.00 I told him he was going to be arrested, and I asked him what unit he was on. He said, "Coffield." I told him, once back at TDC, tell all his homies not to come around northwest Houston, breaking the law. Bad Brad would send them back up I-45. He said okay.

Well, my wife and I were fighting again. I met a dispatcher, and we became friends. I was living in *Tomball*, and she moved in with my sister and got a job at Burger King right down her alley. Sabrina was two, and Sarah was five or six. I got a roommate that was so strange and a loner. His wife died, and it really messed him up. I worked all the time, and my pistol belt never hung there too long. I got a call to my dispatcher's apartment, and she tried to seduce me and had me get her checkbook. She said, "Look inside." It read 130,000. She said, "Leave your wife. We will move to *Kathy*, buy a house, and get married." I said, "Let me think about it." If I had a dollar for every woman that came on to me in uniform, I could have bought a house. Two days later, Sabrina got admitted to the hospital, and I missed two days of work. My friend got mad at me, and that ended our romance. She had done an HPD officer the same way. This lady worked two full-time jobs and was from *Ohio*. My kids were important. She had none, and I told her her money couldn't buy me. *My* wife and I got back together, and I transferred to the mall from *Spring Shadows Glen*.

One night, I took a call with a man running on foot with a gun. I gave chase on foot. We were in a dark alley when he shot at me. I saw the muzzle blast and ducked by a dumpster then shot back and got on the radio. HPD and Harris County came around, and he went to jail. I took a lot of calls, but the two strangest calls follow. A mental resident from the apartment called in. Someone was in his closet. I called for backup, and Tim arrived. We knocked on the door, and a tall black man cracked the door and said he was in the closet and wanted to leave. We checked the apartment. It was clear. He worked for Sears and paid his rent six months ahead. A likable guy. We had gone about twenty minutes and had to come back. I told Tim, "Let me handle it." I went inside

I took vacation and, my first day back, got a call on a shoplifter running toward Gessner. I gave chase, locked my vehicle, and was running; and he had about a seventy-five-yard start on me. Out of the corner of my eye, a sexy lady pulled up and said, "You need a lift?" I said yes. I got on the radio, and backup *was coming*. He went into a bus yard. I thanked the lady and went over the fence. While he was running, he was shooting me the bird. It was funny, and I was pissed and was going to get this panty thief. We searched every bus, finding him hiding under a seat. He had panties, bras, shirts, you name it. He went to jail, and I never would have caught him if that lady wouldn't have stopped. Thank you, whoever you were.

Well, my daughter was getting worse, so I rescinded my position, and we moved back to Palestine. I went to Tyler and got hired on *Lake Palestine Silverleaf Resorts*, patrolling, and worked another security job also. One night on duty, my boss was a prick. He would test me all night long. He had a mounted rattlesnake, hoping I would shoot it. I had my finger on the side of the 357, so it didn't work. He was playing games, and I begged him to fight me. He wouldn't, and I finally quit. I worked my other job, and Joe got me more jobs and security in East Texas, different than Houston. Joe and I got to go to *Lufkin* to watch cars. Real exciting. Joe and I got along. He was an ex–sheriff deputy out of Tyler, had a security car with lights on top, but it was really dirty and had papers on the dash. He told me he had dreams of fixin' it up one day. Then we were sent to Winona Gibraltar *chemical* plant outside of Tyler. This reminds me of the movie, *Silkwood*. The town there was swearing this plant was dumping chemicals into their water system in the ground. The first night I was on duty, I went to one of the two restaurants to get some food. After the last bite, I started throwing up. I talked to the foreman, and he said, "Oh yeah, don't eat at the first place. They don't like us." One late evening, Joe and I was parked in front of the plant, and we heard a long truck with glasspacks coming our way, so we got ready. Two teenagers shot a shotgun toward the plant right over our truck. I heard the BB go over my head. We gave chase, and I called the Sheriff's Department. A deputy was close, and we got them stopped, and they went to jail. They were hired by the town to try to blow up the plant. This was a real war going on; it made the news. They eventually got the plant closed down. One night on duty, I heard someone say, "Open the hatch and dump it." I knew they were dumping chemicals, but I didn't say a word. I acted like I didn't hear that. I met *Sheriff J. B. Smith* at a red light. He said we did a fine job, and he asked me, "When are you going to come to work for me?" I said, "I can't." "Why?" I told him about my dying daughter, and he understood. Law *enforcement* is so exciting and interesting. Once it's in your blood, it stays. In 2000 I went back to TDCJ *Beto*—the young boy's farm.

My outside security experiences 1987–2006

This unit was locked down a lot because these young boys love to fight. On lockdown status, you have to escort them to chow and the shower. We took them to the shower and had no fights. Got back on the wing, and hell broke out. I yelled for them to get in their cells when I saw a Mexican running up the run; he had a weapon. In front of me was a fat black inmate standing there, and before I knew it, he was stabbed ten times. I yelled at the *sergeant* to watch out. I pulled my baton and yelled for him to drop the shank. He did after I hit him once. I handcuffed him and said, "Do you know who I am?" He said no. I said, "*Bad Brad* from *Coffield*," and I said, "Don't you ever stab another inmate right in front of me!" This was over the black offender not paying him a soup he owed him. Damn it. When this happens, you don't think. Your training and body takes over. You are not scared until it is over, then you say, "Shit, I could have gotten killed."

At the next shift briefing, I stood up and asked for donations to repair the sergeant's boots. I had never witnessed a sergeant blow out his boots, keeping me safe. I thanked him, and he said, "*You* handled it, Bad Brad." My last unit was *Ferguson* unit by *Crockett*, Texas, or *Midway*, Texas. Huntsville asked me to go and was shocked when I said yes. They call it the gladiator farm for the shanks and swords that have been found there. The inmates had heard I was coming, and several knew me from Coffield. *They* said they were glad I was there. I liked that old unit; it was like Coffield in a way. I didn't care for the one showboat *warden*. He was in a movie, and I think it went to his head.

One morning, I came in with a small amount of tobacco in my boot. See, in the old days, we could dip and even had spit cans. They changed that, and it caused a lot of problems. The state started treating the employees like criminals. Before I left for good, they even took away their adult books. Well, back to the warden. He was sitting in a chair, going to search some bosses. I didn't want to put it on him, but I had to. I said, "*Good morning, Warden*. You care to search me." He said, "No, Bad Brad. You are okay." I asked again. I said, "Are you sure?" He said, "You're okay!" I went in the restroom and flushed that contraband. I did not trust him as far as I could spit on a windy day.

Shortly after five months, I couldn't take the twelve-hour shifts. I went into Warden Baker's office and resigned, and he said, "If you quit, they won't let you come back." I said, "I won't be back!" I said goodbye to a long, stressful career and will never forget the memories or the people I met. I'd like to say hello to *Stelly*, the man that used to say he could steal my wife away because he was a black man. I enjoyed our talks and jokes about a dream I had. Hope you are out and keeping out of trouble.

From 2003 to 2008, I was a *federal commission security officer.* *Donny Lamb* got me on. Short round was, *the man* worked security all his life!

At first, I was a relief officer. Let's say, someone needed time off, Lieutenant Jones would call me. The hourly rate was good, and they would send us to Louisiana for our training. When the space shuttle blew up, I was in Tyler at a federal building. Lieutenant Jones called and said, "Bad Brad, where are you?" I said, "Are you getting old? Can't you remember?" He said, "Don't be a smart-ass!" *He* was ok, but we had a lot of racial problems. I had heard he had gotten fired for sexual things from TDC, and he was sleeping with the help—a big no-no. He told me the shuttle had blown up and to get home and pack a suitcase. I drove to Houston, and this stupid female that couldn't even shoot got Lieutenant fired, and she didn't let me go. I was so pissed. I filed a suit against *Southwestern Security Services* and won. They owed me travel pay and was keeping work from me.

Once in Louisiana a black supervisor had words with Lieutenant Jones over a female employee, and I wrote up a statement, and it cost me my job. I was relieved of duty in *Mount Pleasant*, Texas. I lasted several years, and I was the youngest, and I was a highway man. I loved that. While on duty in Tyler, I had a mother and daughter attempt to bring in their vibrators. How nasty. We had to search all bags, and you would be surprised what you'd see. I was forty-eight, and I was not planning on retiring. It just happened that way for me. If I had to do it again, I wouldn't change a thing!

Out of all my jobs, I'd say *Rusk State Hospital* was the best for me. I learned about mental issues, about others and me. Bad Brad is alive still, but I'm a lot older now. My diabetes, thyroid, and bipolar is keeping me from working. How long will I live? I'm fifty-four, and I have nothing to prove now. I just want to relax and see if I can live to one hundred years old. Mess with me, my family, or my pride, Bad Brad is coming out! I'm on disability and had a stranger tell me I deserved it after all I did for the state. I draw close to 2,000.00 a month, and I'd like to say thanks to the female *judge* in *Tyler*. Y'all did take care of me. I stay busy, and I love to think back on things. I'm still firm, but fair and have a healthy angel. I'm not too hard on like I was with Sarah. I'm sorry, Sarah, when you believed your mom over the truth. That broke the camel's back. Thanks, Short Round, for being my partner and the long drives. I loved you and *Dusty* like a brother.

CHAPTER 11

My First Divorce and the Scars It Left

The year was May 1987, and my first wife and I tried every-thing to work out our differences, but it was over. I remember the guilt I experienced. I felt like I let myself down, my children, my wife, God; and going to court, watching all those memories fade away, wasn't pleasant. After our hearing, we didn't go by the judge, but she wanted that child support. She was playing games with me, and she was brainwashing *Sarah* against me. It worked still as today. Sarah and I aren't close, and we never will be. I will never forget a guy named *David*, and she was telling him a pack of lies. It took years, but her lies finally got back around, and the truth set me free. I was paying her child support, $350.00 a month, and seeing my girls, but deep down I wanted my innocent wife back.

After time, I realized, due to my relationship with my mother, it helped in the causes of my *divorce*. I started being a woman hater. I was jumping from woman to woman, looking for someone to take my pain away. It wasn't working. I was unstable on my jobs and mak-ing bad decisions. A little time went by, and due to our sick daughter, I told my ex, no other man would want to be with her.

One afternoon, I was sitting on my couch, and my phone rang. It was her. She had blown up my truck and wanted me to come get

48

her. I went—another mistake—but I cared. I guess because she was the girls' mom. Before I knew it, we were sleeping together, and no birth control or control on my part. She got pregnant. When you get hurt and you have both been with others, things change. It haunts your mind. You feel different, and nothing really changed except, when you fight, you use those weapons to hurt one another.

I started dating a woman that had the same name as my ex. It worked. It drove her crazy. After five months, I caught her shaking my little angel, *Samantha*. I grabbed her and told her not to do it again and to call her dad and to get out of my trailer. She left and got a lawyer, trying to put it on me. I hired my attorney, and the judge ruled we go our separate ways. She was a winner. She had lied about how many times she married, and I was glad I ran her off. I guess I look for love in all the wrong places. My other relationships from *Troup* and *Grapeland* ended in heartache. Now in 2008 I finally learned not to jump into a quick marriage. In Texas it is easy to marry, but harder to get a divorce without losing and having to start over. I think your credit suffers the most. I wouldn't have married so many times if I could do it again. Out of all my wives, the one from Troup stands out in my heart I guess because we hunted and fished, and she crosses my mind a lot. For the others, they were mistakes. I'm sorry I hurt y'all for something that happened to me when my parents divorced. The endless cycle never ends. If your parents fight and divorce, it can affect you dearly.

C H A P T E R   1 2

Being Admitted to Rusk State Hospital

The year was 2000. What a bad year I had. A divorce, my dad died, my daughter left my house, and I got locked up for two weeks in the crazy house. I think back on the stress I was under and the toll it had on my health. I had hurt my back at *Walmart* and was on workers' comp for the second time. My ex was trying to keep my kids from me, and I took a picture of us and shot it with my .22. I had run out of targets. I hit her twenty times, and it felt good. She called, fighting, and I told her what I did, and she was dead to me. It scared her. She called my mother and sister, then *Shelly* went to the judge and got a warrant to have me checked out. They did me a favor but was sneaky about it. Honestly, I was thinking about hurting her. She had another man in my trailer and wouldn't leave me alone. I did not have a nervous breakdown, she did. I was suffering from no sleep and depression and anger issues. After the hospital, I'm not sure what happened, but I was depressed and was having severe mood swings. After some meds, I started getting better. I leveled out and realized I had to let her go. Once she was my oxygen. I accepted my failures and the past. I got out, hired my lawyer, and I hated the woman I once loved so much. I was out for blood and was going to get her by telling the truth. I won my five acres, trailer, and my daughter *Sarah*. My back got better, and I went back to work. My only regret to the past was that my daughter got used as a bridge.

CHAPTER 13

Learning About Mental Illness: Depression and Being Bipolar

I got out, and I asked Randy, a PSY, how long I had to wait until I could apply for a job. He said six months. I went and applied for housekeeping job. After a while, I transferred in as a service assistant who takes care of the patients. After a while, I saw a lot of my own behaviors in my patients. I did a lot of reading up on bipolar. Bad Brad got known around the grounds. They would call on me when a patient would want to fight the staff. At first, I was working on a female unit. I liked it but wasn't used to being around those girls.

One day, I had a black patient take an extension cord. After the head nurse and I was called in to defuse her. I walked in and asked for the cord. She said, "Bad Brad, I was waiting on you, and you're not that bad." Luckily, security got behind her, and she tried to hit me. I grabbed her hand, bent her finger, and she went in the padded room. People with mental issues have a great strength physically. I witnessed a young twenty-year-old male rip a double door off the hinges.

I worked there for three years and got employee of the month and year. I took vacation. My sister, Sarah, and Samantha got to go to *Disney World* in *Florida*. We had a blast and got to go to the head of the lines on all rides. When I came back, I got to go to MDU with males and females. I learned a lot about mental illness and would have stayed, but we didn't get a pay raise. They paved the roads and got new vans. My daughter got sick, and I had to go on family leave, and my ex lied about me not being at hospital. I was living in Troup was very happy. We were going in the evenings. I got called in to HR, and the director acted ugly toward me. I met with my supervisor and quit. I was shocked when they knew my child was dying. A while later, Samantha lost her battle with her illness. I went to work for *Dunbar* as an armed money carrier. I will never forget *Rusk*, and I know I helped a lot of the patients there. It almost got closed down in 2005, but they fought, and it stayed opened. In 2006 I went back and started orientation but changed my mind and went home. I couldn't go back.

CHAPTER 14

Moving to Houston

My world came crashing down. Shortly after my daughter's death, I was forced to go to court and fight for custody of my son, Shane.

After months of hard work, my attorney told me to keep him on my next visit. Janet and I painted a house in Troup and made $2,500.00, and it all went to my attorney. I got put on stand for two hours, and they tried to make me out to be a bipolar, monster dad. Their testimony was a pack of lies. My ex lies so much she wouldn't know the truth if it touched her on the butt. I told the truth, and it set us free. After the verdict, I won full custody of *Shane Dakota Bradley*. We went to my grandmother's home, where Shane was staying. I told her about all the lies that was told on my good character, and we laughed our asses off.

We went home, and for six months, we were very happy. I had her and her uneducated family and friends where they needed to be—beneath me. My wife lost her job at *Family Dollar*, and she was a stressed-out woman. The love she had for us disappeared out of her eyes. She was in debt on twelve credit cards, and I figured I gave her $12,000.00 over five years, and it didn't put a dent in her balances. My world came crashing down, and I assumed we were going to be together forever. Boy, I was wrong.

One weekend, I figured out the bills and her indebtedness. $32,000.00. She said she was in for $ 98,000.00, and she was blaming me. Shit, she was in deep when I first met her with her golden credit. She and I sat down, and I told her if I took down one mounted stuffed animal off the wall and leave, my pride wouldn't let me come back. She better think about it. She left for her sister's in Marshall, Texas. Shane and I packed up and left. I think she was listening to everyone but me. I couldn't believe how she hurt Shane when she promised him we would always be a family.

I called my sister, and we headed for Kathy, outside Houston. Shane and I cried all the way to Huntsville. Once there, I went and got a great *security* job. My sister was raising my son, and I wanted to go back to how things were six months ago. One late night, I came in and got out of my uniform, and she called me, crying. I thought maybe she had come to her senses. I was wrong. She said she couldn't stop thinking of me but didn't want me back. She hired a lawyer. She wanted the truck and boat back. I told her I'd see her in court and not to call me anymore. I hired *Mark*, paid him, and told him I was ready to fight her. Every other weekend, I was driving to Crockett to drop off Shane to my first ex-wife, and that was killing me. I decided to move back to Palestine. Luckily, I spoke to Donny, and he gave us a place to live. He was a true friend.

We went to court, and she tried to make me pay for her mistakes. It didn't work. You should have seen the *judge's* mouth drop when my attorney told him about the $98,000.00 debt. I started to laugh, but when I go to court —— her credit cards. I lost out on so much money, my wife, my best friend, love, and so much more. I'm still not over that chapter in my life. She and I had it all, and it was over in a blink of an eye. She lost her job, her mind, and her credit, and us. If you ever read this, I was your everything, and you hurt two people that really loved you, and I'm so sorry you did not save yourself and us. At our hearing, she tried to talk to Shane, and he turned his head and walked on by. I was proud of him. It was hard, but I went on without her. For a long time, for years, she would cross my mind daily. For years and still today, I don't know why she turned on me. I never hit her, screwed around on her. I guess she just changed.

In the end, she judged me about being *bipolar*. Her thyroid didn't work, and I guess I opened my eyes about her. She was a man-hater because of what *Jack*, her first, did to her. She had scars, and I guess a lot of people never get over things. She had a smile that could melt you down. I wonder if I ever cross her mind. I haven't talked to her and don't plan on it. I hope she learned you don't base your happiness on a credit card.

C H A P T E R   1 5

My Only Sister, Dawn Renee Bradley

My sister was born January 9, 1968, in Houston at St. Joseph's Hospital. When we were little, we were so close. For a while, I lived in Franklin, and she stayed in Houston. I remember pulling up to 6832 Ave I, and she would come running, yelling, "Doguie." I'd get out of the car and run to her and say, "Dawnie."

She had a few close calls when she was a little girl. One time, she swallowed a Blow Pop, and it got caught in her throat. Granny had to turn her upside down and shake it loose. She had a black tumor on her chest and had it removed. In the seventies, she had a car wreck and broke her leg in two places and had to learn to walk again. When she got older, she became a redheaded rebel without a cause. She went man-crazy and ran off to *Dallas, Texas*, with *Chris*, our cousin. She and I are totally different. Like night and day. I'm going to try not to throw her under the bus, but I have to tell the truth and how I see it through my blue eyes.

She always had a problem with telling the truth. I don't understand that. Yes, I do, maybe because dad wasn't as hard on her. Growing up off Wayside, she was my shadow. One time, we were sent on our bikes to the market for milk. There was a concrete lip, and she tried to raise her front wheel and crashed, hitting her head on a concrete wall. She cried and said, "Doguie." I felt so sorry for her.

After my children were born, she took up with them and other friends' kids. I guess because she never had kids of her own. After my first divorce, she finally opened her eyes about my ex. Today she has blond hair, but she still acts like a real redhead. She has a fire streak that runs down her spine. All the fights we've had, she will never swallow her pride and apologize. She has other problems I can't mention, but everyone does. She used to judge me. She says it's out of love, but I look at it differently. She used to hurt me with her mouth, and in my opinion, she is too controlling at times. She is like my mother, and I have both traits running through my veins.

In 2008 she married a guy I couldn't stand. Still today she won't listen, and I'm the older sib. They finally divorced, and I guess when she has enough, she is done. I say we are different, but are we? I've been her older brother, and I wanted to be her protector, but she is too proudful, and sometimes we clash. She seems to always take up for the woman, and I stay neutral. When Mom was sick, I was afraid she did what she did for the money, but that wasn't the case. She treated me fairly, and she was honest. I was proud, and we both needed closure. I love my sister, but I have always had problems, and I deal with them cold turkey. We have both made mistakes and had to live with them. I tried to be her rock, but now that I'm older and retired, I need a rock. I wish her well, and I do love her.

CHAPTER 16

My Great-Grandmother Juanita Shelton

My grandmother was born in *Oklahoma* and only had a sixth-grade education. She used to walk five miles to and from school in the rain, heat, and snow. She grew up with the Indians, and she used to tell me stories about life. One story that sticks out was when she was walking home, and something was following her in the brush. She made it home, told her dad and uncle. They saddled up and went back to find and killed a large cougar. She was lucky, and why he or she didn't attack is beyond me. That cat was nine feet long. She was a survivor and one hell of a woman.

She educated herself by reading all kinds of books. She was, like me, a rolling stone and lived different places. She was married nine times. Had me beat by four, and I asked her one time, "Why so many?" She said, back in the day, people would disown you if you weren't married, and she didn't take any shit off a man. What's my excuse? Until *Donna*, I've never have had anyone stand beside me. I was like, "Ma, I looked at it like I could replace them, and I did. I just don't put up with their shit." I've changed that thinking. Got tired of paying my lawyer.

For years, she drank beer and smoked and would fight the devil just to have something to do. No lie, she was tough. Once at bingo,

59

she put her best friend's head in the toilet for talking shit about her. *Wow*. I think me and my cousin *Bryan* would do the same. She was a mother, a friend, grandmother, fighter, not a holy woman, and she loved deeply. I guess I got my craziness from her.

Growing up as a teenager, we had fun, but I admit it she did spoil me and others. Certain people were jealous of this. No names mentioned. You know who you are. She just loved boys properly because she lost *Gray* and carried the guilt because she was drinking and blamed herself for his death. I can relate to that since I've lost two daughters and really lost my other kids since we never talk.

When I worked at Coffield, I watched her beat her last husband, James, with a frozen loaf of bread. He was messing with my two young cousins, and she would whop you over us kids. She wore the pants, and my grandfather was weak! Bryan/Brent became her favorite, and I was okay with that I had my turn. My aunt took care of her and did a fine job. We all did our part, and I wish she was there and here with us all.

It seemed weird when she went to the nursing home! Then when her house was gone, that sucked! But nothing stays the same. I moved away, but in my mind, I will always remember her and the fifteen acres—the way it was when they first got it in Palestine. I would visit her, and she didn't want to be in that home, but it was best, and she kept them all walking a straight line. For years, she rocked on. She was on a lot of meds.

In *October* I got the call she was at the end of her road. I rushed up to her; she was waiting for me. I walked in, and *Shelly* and *Dawn* were crying. I took her hand and told her to go to the light, my girls are waiting. She took that last breath, and a goodbye tear came down. Bad Brad helped me that day, but it was very hard letting her go. I cried. I lost a mother, a friend, and a grandmother that day. I went home to Donna. She was at the hospital with our daughter *Savannah Nicole Bradley*. Three days later, on October 21, 2013, my angel was born. My last chance to be another father. Maybe I will get it right. I wish Ma could have held her. She was born on the same day I had lost another angel, just a different year. I believed God gave me one back since I lost two in the past. What a blessing! One great person dies, and another is born. I can't wat t to see Ma again and all my relatives. If I make it to heaven one day. We really loved each other the right way, and that is how God intended love to be. She was the best grandmother a little boy could wish for. I hope all my family realize she loved us all just in her own way. She was always there for me because she knew I didn't have a real, real mother! Thanks for being my friend.

C H A P T E R   1 7

Best Friends

Best friends are like the number of cars you've owned since you graduated from high school. For me, I've had about five.

Steve is my longest friend. We got into trouble when we were in high school, breaking into Waltrip High, steeling *gym* clothes. Sorry I snitched, but I was trying to save myself. Didn't want to go to jail. Cannot imagine going with blue eyes and a sexy butt. LOL. Get r done. Ha! Ha! That is some funny stuff! Then we started dating girls. Sorry, Johnny Cash's daughter, Terry, didn't work out for you. At least I tried to set you up. You were so shy. I had never flirted with anyone on the highway. That was cool. Then I helped with your best friend, *Beth*. You owe me $99.00. I accept Visa or Mastercard. Haha! We have had years of deer-hunting memories from moving stands, you earning your nickname, "Gut shoot 'em up Charlie," and going to *Columbus*, attempting to save a shot doe and almost getting shot. That was your idea. No, I can't lie. I think it was mine. I'm sorry I've tried to be your best friend. Up and away. What about the time the cougar was in the area, and at dusk you jumped out and scared me. Damn it, boy, don't do that at fifty-four. I might quit breathing, and since I dip, I don't think you would give me mouth to mouth. We have had so many good times, and in my eyes, you are a superfine guy. I hope you hunt with me until the day I either quit or die one. Hope you get a big buck. Let's keep building memories.

Then there was John. He was a super-loyal friend, and we had a lot of memories, and he was a crazy white boy. I spoke a lot about him in another chapter, so I will make it short. Donny Lamb was my partner, only one I had, and we were there for each other; and his son was my skirt-chasing friend in between my marriages. He always had more beer, but someone had to drive, and that was me, Bad Brad. Everyone will not be your best friend. Shit, some people won't even be a friend. My last and final wife, Donna, tells me we are best friends I don't know about that. Soulmates, yes! So if you have a best friend, work on it and show and tell them how grateful you are to have them in your life.

CHAPTER 18

Leaving Grapeland in a Cloud of Dust?

The year was 2008, and boy, I was having a bad year. After all I did for my wife, saving her life, she turned out to be so selfish and a gold digger. I lost my mom to *cancer*, lost my disability case, and was unhappy and depressed. I lost my son. He got out of the bull-shit, and Shane, I'm sorry for any hurt I caused you. What comes up must come down. I was in a spiral, hitting the ground hard. My marriage was over, and I wish I had never felt sorry for this abused country girl. I went to Brent's and borrowed some money and told him I had enough, and I needed to leave Grapeland in a —— duat, and I was ending my marriage. I hated that time and the town and disliked my wife. It has been years, and went over there, and nothing has changed. It's only a good place to live if you want to grow water-melons. Oh yes, or peanuts.

C H A P T E R   1 9

Struggling to Get Back in the Middle

I think when I left Grapeland, Texas, in 2008, my ex put a hex—Indian type—on me. No matter how hard I tried to get stable, something would happen to knock me down again. I tried living with my sister in Pearland—bad idea—and the only positive thing I had in my corner was my health, and I was working security for NASA and a full-time job at *Baybrook* Mall as a *sergeant*.

I lived out of motels for a while, and when you get right down to your problems, no one really cares. I was homeless, and I did not enjoy that. I'd like to thank *Outlaw* in *Groveton* for trying to help me. My cousins spoke with me on the phone and gave me advice, and their opinion, it didn't fix my problem quickly. I guess I brought this on myself, but I wanted back in the middle and needed to be happy. Paul in Cleveland, Texas, was a good friend and a great help. Thanks, Paul. If you ever need me, please call on old Bad Brad. We worked at the private prison and were roommates for a while. Then a woman got involved, and it was time to move on down the road. My stepbrother and Sonny let me stay with him for a while, and it brought back good memories for me when I was in high school. Those were the days.

In 2011 I choice a new career path. I went to Dallas to a CDL course. Graduation came, and I was a truck driver for the United States of America. I tried to like it, but living out of a truck and the poor pay was killing me. The country was beautiful, especially West Virginia. God put me on a path to meet my mentor and the best trainer, Donny. We had a safe blast, and you know me. I had to tell him all about Bad Brad. After four months, he almost had me as a truck driver, but I ran low on my thyroid medicine, and I was super tired and getting sleepy behind the wheel of that big rig, so I decided to step off his truck in May 2011. I had no regrets, and I think he understood. We are good friends still today, and I will sum him up to size. He is the finest *Christian* I know, and he is *the* man. I went to the doctor and got better.

I was missing law enforcement and a lot of other things, but God had plans for me. I moved in with Donna, was doing yard work, and I applied for a roll-off truck job in Pasadena off Spencer and got the job. I was in the money, and finally, I was getting back in the middle. I was happy, and I loved the hours and the job. Thanks, Randy, for taking a chance on me. You are the best. We had the customers. I delivered sawdust, pallets, and was a team player. I bought a bike, car, and found my soulmate, Miss Donna. Then in February 2013 I went to the take my DOT physical, so I couldn't work for Randy. I was crushed. I went to the VA, and I had *diabetes*. So I turned in the paperwork to the *social security*, and they took care of me. I got my disability. I was about time. Praise.

Donna and I went to the park and had a heart-to-heart about our future plans. We had a house full of people, including her three grown kids, and no privacy, but we were having fun. She worked for the Port of Houston, and on the weekends, we would go either the Galveston or Crystal Beach. I was tempted, and one or maybe three were trying to run me off. Nana, my ex-mother-in-law, got on the computer and did a background check on me. What a joke! I had told Donna about my past, and I was once upon a time a *private investigator* in Houston and did not check any of them out because I was afraid of what I could have dug up.

Donn's daughters, little Nick, and I had a talk about our relationship, and I saw through Donna's kids the past hurt coming forward about Donna's divorce from their father, the Laporte police officer. That happened in 1997. One grown daughter told me they were a package deal, and I knew they were jealous, and I fell in love with Donna so much I knew Bad Brad could handle without running off and without hurting Miss Donna. I was trying to get to know her children and earn their respect. I don't think it worked, but at least I tried. I went to one of Donna's daughters and cared enough to talk to her about mental illness. It was like talking to a deaf person.

Donna's oldest daughter friend was very likable person, and it wasn't anything personal, but Donna and I were tired of too many personalities in the home, so it was time for us all to go our separate ways. I went off, and my bad side came out, and I told the friend it was time for them to find their own place. I'm sorry I hurt you, and I left that night went to meet Cedric at a club. I didn't want to lose Donna, but too much drama. Donna was losing her house, and we were trying to figure out where we were going to live. One daughter begged me to call her mom and stay together. I called, and Donna was upset and crying, and we worked it out. Driving home that morning at 2:00 a.m., I fell asleep and had another motorist say, "Are you okay?" I woke up, and I was going thirty miles an hour on a major freeway. I woke up, and an angel was in the car with me. Made it back to my Miss Donna's arms.

We moved in with her daughter, and that worked out for a while. We went to a small motel, and we were comfortable, then we got us a FEMA trailer, moved to Baytown, and Donna became pregnant. We stayed there six months, and we had had enough and was ready for the country life, so I went to Woodville, and baby Savanah Bradley was the highlight of our life together. Donna resigned her position, and I had to watch the baby for two weeks. I had no major issues, but I was a rusty dad, and the day Mom came home to join us. I was so relieved. We stayed there, and then we tried to buy a small place in Ivanhoe, outside Woodville. My neighbor was Big Jimmy, an older convict that is like me, has a lot of knowledge and street smarts. Let the trailer go since owner was nickel and diming us to death. We went back to the park and loved Donna working in the office for the owner. We loved that park and the owner like a father.

After one year, it was time to move. We went to Livingston, Texas, a place that is okay, but I couldn't understand how I ended up back where I had been several years before. We stayed with a good friend. My sister stepped in and allowed us to borrow her and Larry's RV. We bought a used RV, and we went to Bustertown in Livingston. *Wanted* to move by my deer lease off Tom Cummins RD and enjoyed that until the fleas took us away. Donna wanted to be closer to her sister and family, so I said, what the hell, I'm a highway man. Let's move again. We went on that 1,500-mile ride with only money and our suitcases. (Damn it) I need to seek medical help. I was Texas homesick. God helped us. We made it home safely and stayed at Cowboy's trailer, or our old RV that we sold to him. I prayed to my boss, and we went to Julie, the sweetest lady in Coldspring, Texas. We are buying a nice trailer, and we all want to stay married and love the RV park. I want to thank my big and first boss, *God*, and Donna and I are glad were strong, and one thing I love about Donna—she stands by her man—and I have never had it is so nice. Nick is training me, and I'm training him, and both are the apple of my blue eyes. Donna gave up on her disabilities, and I'm trying to enjoy my retirement, but my wife, kids, and myself won't allow it. I think the Lord, and us *Bradleys* are going to stay strong and serve the Lord and enjoy Texas and my family. *God bless Texas* and this great country we love and will defend to the end.

C H A P T E R   2 0

Dealing with Stress and My Demons

I've had stress in my life since 1988. I know, either from getting hit in the head while from the prison or the loss of my two beautiful daughters, it caused a chemical imbalance in my brain. I can feel the change coming on when I get super stressed out. And even with my medicines (three) I take, it levels it out, but doesn't make it go away until the cycle ends. After my daughters' death, time, prayer, and the woods helped me, but the depression was still there. It hits me hard now only once in a while. I get mood swings, and I'm a Gemini. I don't hear voices, only my wife, and she is nothing like me. I do hear bells or a loud ringing in my head. I become overtalkative, and I do that because I think I'm trying to get the stress out. I have the great energy for a while, and then I crash with no energy, and I'm real quiet. Why did this happen to me? I don't know, but I do know it is something that a lot of people judge you about. Mental illness is like the universe. It is to be explored and to try to understand, not judge or change.

When I was younger, I had two sides, had no manic or depression. I think too much stress in my life brought this on. I get quiet and don't care; that is my way I am thinking about things in my life. I'm not crazy, just me. I love to fish and hunt. It gives me the chance to do something different, and I guess it relaxes me. In 2012 I finally realized stress is Bad Brad's number one enemy, not an offender. I

69

slammed at Coffield off of L wing in 1988. A doctor told me I'd be dead in a few years if I didn't control my stress factor, so I changed a lot, but I strongly feel I will die when I decide and when it's my turn. You go first. I think I will hang in the for the long haul.

In today's society, we all have stress. The world and a lot of the people in it have let the stress make them crazy. With Donna, we had a lot of stress. We had stress and drama, but I handled it, and the demon was dead, and I put some distance between us and them. My demon starts out with yelling, then my demon goes to one hundred in minutes, then I get physical, then I know I'm not weak in my opinion. Bad Brad is out. I'm not superman, but I am bad to the bone, and *I'm* proud to be known as the real Bad Brad that fell off the Coffield Unit. I have learned to live right with God first. He should always be number one. Eat right, stay focused, be positive, and rest when you are tired. Love yourself regardless what mistakes you make, and hope God gives you another day to enjoy his creations. Oh yeah, if you can't handle a demon, call on me. I bet you Bad Brad can. Forgive yourself about the past, live each day to the fullest, and have fun. If you make it to veteran status, it is all downhill from there. I know I was Bad Brad but only when I had to be.

C H A P T E R   2 1

Going on Disability, Hanging Up My Uniform, and Retiring My Badge (210)

Well, the year was 2008. I left Grapeland and went to borrow $200 from my cousin. I went to Houston and stayed with my sister. Got two security jobs, one for NASA security and a patrol officer at Baybrook Mall, located off 45 in Webster, Texas.

I loved my job, and after three months of showing my true colors, I made supervisor Buck Sergeant.

After a while, a year and a half, or eighteen months, my mental health was getting worse. I was working all holidays, and eight to twelve hours a day. I got my divorce behind me and lost myself and son along the way. I had truck problems for a week and finally went in to the mall, turned in my equipment badge, and quit.

I cried like a baby.

Still today I miss the uniform badge, pistol belt, and my Smith & Wesson 357. I loved being the good guy and serving the public.

Searching for peace

Well, I've been searching for peace really all my life, but all my drama started in 1987, or let's just say way, way back there, to be honest. I've found some all portions of it. For example: You're in a deer stand, and a healthy doe with two fawns come slowly walking by, and you speak to them softly and say, "You are safe," and they don't blow at you and run off. A magnificent sunset on a beautiful lake or a pasture of Indian paint brushes. A daughter or son is born too. You and they are healthy. You're in your bass boat on *Lake Palestine* early in the dawn hours, going forty miles per hour, looking for a honey hole, and the water is like glass. Peace can't be bought at Walmart, can't be borrowed. It has to come from you, and it is sometimes deep, deep down. Through prayer, *God*, our Maker, can give you this, but you have to do your part.

I had no guilt and had peace when I lost my two daughters. Didn't want to lose them, but my peace was, I did not have to see them cry or suffer anymore. It broke my heart into little pieces, but time and God helped me survive and put my heart back together again so I could live on. Certain people blamed me, the good guy, and that was okay. I knew it wasn't all my fault in the end; we were both carrying this rare disease. She cussed God one night, and I took a slap in the face and did not hit her back. I prayed and begged and asked God to save them and take me home instead.

I was baptized at park Memorial Baptist Church off Wayside Drive in Houston in the seventies. I was seven years old, I believe, and I was forced to go on *Wednesdays* and *Sundays*, and I was so thankful because it opened my young mind up to a lot of things. I believe in a lot of things: God, Satan, Bigfoot, aliens, doing the right thing, my country—even though it is not always right—and other things that a lot of people will argue or fight you just to be talking to you just to prove a negative point. I've been dealing with all kinds of people most of my adult life, and I don't understand them. I think I understand more why a *grizzly* will eat you than I do about what people say and do. The answer to the bear: (1) he is hungry, (2) you are in his territory, and that's what a (3) bear is supposed to do. I'm still struggling to get 100 percent of peace in my life before I die. One day I will do it, you bet. Having faith in yourself and leaving the past behind is my recipe. So many of us, all races, paint an untrue picture of us and others, judge one another, and live in sin, hide it, and hope no one ever finds out. God knows all things, and if you know the difference between good and evil, right or wrong, that makes you a good person and a good lady or a real good man. That's my verdict. Going to church helps. It is a place to worship God, not to be a devil, and you're going to use the pastor because he is a giver with the offering plate. Living for God is the answer.

C H A P T E R   2 2

Being Positive and Never Giving Up

After all I've been through, I wonder how I turned out positive or alive. I guess anyone can turn any situation around if you
try hard enough. That's what I did. I've been negative and never
wanted anyone to feel sorry for me, judge my words or my actions.
We are all different, and I think that is so, so cool. While at Rusk
State Hospital, I had to evaluate myself and everything in my life to
accept my problems to get better. I had a lot of help. Then I turned
it around, went there and helped others, and did the same at *Mexia
State School.* Boy, that was a long drive each day. I accept everything
today. I believe in two sayings. (1) Let go and let *God* handle it. (2)
It is what it is. Accept it, or be man enough to change it. I know a
lot of people in my blue book. I have never met the preacher, *Mr.
Joel Olsten*, but I do know I'm a great listener and fair talker. His dad
through the holy spirit allowed this great man to carry on the words
to help save people. That is a great, great thing. *You go.* You have my
vote. We all have jobs, and when you have a job, do it well. That's
what I did. I was a little to positive and blew out my thyroid. Thank
goodness for the right pill. It will all come out in the wash. When?
Only God has that answer. At fifty-four, I think I will stay sharp as
my knife when the time is right. *I will. I promise I will* do my part
positively. When I drive in all areas, I see signs that say and mean dif-

74

ferent things about God coming back soon. I say a silent prayer *and* I say, "Heavenly Father, whenever you're ready, call on me, Bad Brad, I will do whatever you want. Amen." I hope he hears me.

C H A P T E R   2 3

Looking Back on the Past

Well, I'm ending my book, and I'm really tired, so, everyone, bear with me. It's time to call in the hog dogs, put out the fire, and let the past be that—*the past!* When you get older, you look back, and you think about so much; and you are cross-eyed, your brain is swollen, and you say, "I made it!" I regret so much: marrying too much, not becoming a *peace* officer, not living in the *wild, wild west,* and losing angels along the way. Most of my life, I was a rolling stone. That was my way, and that wasn't against the law, so if you don't like it, don't read my story. If you do buy this great book, and I'm still walking on stability and got to raise credit score to get my VA loan. Hurry up, *Bad Brad,* you're getting old. I should have been more stable. I wish I would have met *Miss Donna* back in 1982. I could have been a deacon in the church. I guess I am a dreamer. Would rather dream good and long rather than bad and short dreams. It is amazing how the American dream has stayed alive all these years. I have no regrets about my life, and I'm not a loser, just God only made one of me. I'm not greedy. I want to tell the truth about my book and have the chance to express myself. I'm not the sharpest knife in the kitchen drawer, but don't leave me out in the yard. I'm not the most educated man; at least I wanted an associate's degree, and I've done my part in the end. Well, we will see. I've been called the man also. I used to be a little boy. It is hard to go from a boy to a man. Y'all take a break. Smoke 'em if you have 'em. Thank you for listening.

CHAPTER 24

Starting Over at Fifty

Well, this will be a long, draining, filled chapter, but I will get it done. I'll stick to the story, the truth, and the facts. I wouldn't want my readers to say behind my back that I was full of crap or a drama king. I'm not a hater to everyone. I'll just say, don't tread on me. I do dislike people that feed off drama, hate, and the past. Some go beyond the call of duty not to listen, understand others, or they say I will not or I'm not changing. Anyone or anything can change. Instead of God putting me, Bad Brad, with someone that needed my help, he gave me two people that he knew could help me. One was Miss Donna Gallion back then and good Donny USA, my mentor. No words or money can express my gratitude to express my thanks.

Donna is sharp when she wants to be, tired 80 percent, my soulmate, and we have loved a lifetime, and I want to be laid beside her in a small country plot in Cleveland, and I don't ever want to start over at fifty-four, fifty-eight, nor will I ever lose out or harm her deeply like I did in my past. I will and cannot let her mom down. I am a man of my word 80 percent of the time; the other 20 percent is only because we all live in a fast-paced world, and it's getting harder and harder to keep your word these days. Donna has taught me to love unconditionally, to listen to her, not to leave her behind, to be a good husband and just be me. She will always be my number one, even if she has no makeup on, no money, or no teeth.

As for Donny USA, it's really simple. I'm sorry I had to tell you my life stories, but I did not lie or use you. I wanted you to decide if I was truck-driving material. In the end, Bad Brad did his part, and I hated to step off your great truck. I did it for us, but I couldn't forget about you. Sometimes starting over is a great thing. My goal is not to allow myself to go back to 1982 and start over, but I will accept what I have to, and I will change *myself* and continue to accept and never judge anyone. Bad Brad—let's all allow him to *rest*. He is super, super, super tired. Amen and God bless.

C H A P T E R   2 5

Living My Dream

Well, it's 2022, and I've been super busy. I have been busy managing 340 acres on my deer lease. I have six hunters under me, and they all have different needs that I have to handle. I love doing it, and it keeps me moving and fighting my diabetic condition. Donna and I have been married for eight years. We are happy buying our large mobile home and four acres. Her health is getting worse, and in my opinion, I'm catching up to her. In July she had stomach surgery and has lost forty pounds. I don't know how this will affect us, but I guess I will find out soon enough. Been busy with my sixteen-year-old son, Nick. Donna's and Nick's birthday is June 26, 2021. Yeah, both were born on June 26. How weird. Donna and I bought Nick a $2,500.00 Chevy Trailblazer SUV, and we gave him a surprise birthday party. We invited twenty people, but only ten people showed up for the party.

Nick has fallen behind in school. I have to constantly stay on him about his grades, work around the house, and go to school. I don't understand these kids today. They only want to play video games and keep their noses and ears stuck to a phone. When I was growing up, it was out of sight, *out of mind.*

We had to play outside. I did a variety of different things, like baseball, football, swimming on hot summer days, dirt bikes, fishing, and exploring girls.

I always had fun and stayed out of trouble; Nick is the opposite. I took on raising him from five years old, and it's been hard. Teenagers go through so much, and as a father, sometimes I don't understand Nick or how to handle Nick and my daughter, Savannah Nicole Bradley, eight years old. My wife and I and my sister have spoiled our daughter.

She is the apple of both my blue eyes, but honestly, I'll be glad when they are grown.

Savannah is my last healthy daughter, and she gives me a reason to live until she is eighteen.

New Year's Eve 2022

This is going to be my *year*. I have almost everything a man wants and needs.

My wife and I, Pedro and Michelle, and Lisa and Larry all met at a sports bar located on Spencer Highway in Pasadena, Texas, home of Urban Cowboy and Gilley's—which is not there anymore, but the memories of the hottest honky-tonk live on.

At sixteen years old, my mother was doing carpet jobs for Mickey Gilley, and she got me in one weekend. Girls everywhere. I rode the bull, but no beer-drinking.

Well, back to New Year's Eve 2022. We had a blast. I sang three songs and got a good buzz going and brought in the new year with my wife and friends. Donna drove me home since I was drunk. We made it home safely around 3:00 a.m.

The next morning, I woke up with a slight hangover and didn't do much. Well, the next day, went to the store and met a homeless lady—let's call her Susan. Gave her money, bought her a jacket and purse, and even got her a job cleaning Mr. Snook's *mansion*.

Was going to get her out of the Livingston Shelter and let her stay with us for a while. Well, to make a long story short, she transferred to the Huntsville Shelter. Her phone got cut off, and she stood Donna up twice. That was it. God expects us to help the less fortunate.

Some people get down in life and don't want to help themselves. In 2008 I was homeless, living out of my truck, working security in

Lufkin, bouncing around from motel to motel, and staying with a friend, Bobby. I finally called my stepbrother, Mark, and stayed with him until I got up on my feet.

Then after a few dates, I moved in with Miss Donna. Donna and I went on disability and got to retire. Now I have a stable home, two paid-off vehicles, good retirement income, two healthy kids, and my best friend and soulmate.

God is so good.

"For God so loved the world he gave his only begotten son and whom ever shall believe in him shall not perish, but have everlasting life" (John 3:16).

My favorite verse.

Helping another homeless person

Well, God works in mysterious ways. I met a man—let's call him Joe—and he was living in the woods, then he moved in a horse trailer. I wanted to hire him to trim the fences on my four acres. I allowed him to shower, but after a short time, he had a drinking problem. I was going to help him get a small truck and RV.

He was a likable guy, but he didn't want to work.

It was getting to the point where he would call, asking for a ride or money. I feel like God would bless me for being kind.

Finally, I had enough. He would get his check and go to the motel. I met him at the store and got the money I lent him. I had to tell him this wasn't working out. He said he understood.

Christmas 2021

Well, it's Christmastime. My favorite holiday. I put Christmas lights on the front porch. Next year, I'd love to go to Walmart and buy three blow-up things for the front yard.

Savannah and I went to Hobby Lobby and bought twenty-five paper angels, and we put up an "angel tree," with all our fallen deceased family members. It was beautiful. When I think of Christmas, I think of my first daughter, Sarah. I was in Germany, and they brought her to me in a Christmas stocking. It was weird being at the hospital instead of being in bed, waiting on Santa to arrive. Nick got his first vehicle. I was sixteen years old when Sonny bought me my first vehicle. It was a 1982 Dodge half-ton pickup.

Savannah got a lot of different things, Donna got a new wedding ring, and I got a new watch. I'm hoping next Christmas, after my book comes out, we all can get one big present.

Getting my book published—my birthday present to myself

Well, I'm super excited about going to New York City or Pennsylvania in June for my contract signing and picture-taking for the front cover; however, I'm a little nervous about going to NYC as a cowboy.

I think I will hide my straw hat and buy an NYC ball cap so I can blend in. I don't want to get robbed or stabbed or shot. We will be there for three days, and my security side will be on full alert. I'm bringing my badge. Well, if my book does well, there will be *one* more book. It will be called *The Texas Outdoors Man*." I've been working in security for twenty-four years. I relied on fishing and hunting to relieve my stress. So I'm writing about my hunting and fishing memories.

Friends and family

When a man is young, he only thinks about partying and women. Being wild and drinking.

When a man reaches fifty years old, he looks back on his life and laughs at his mistakes.

My mistakes were marrying my ex-wives. I know now I married the wrong women. I should have broken up with them and driven off into the sun. Friends and family are very important. I've had a lot of friends, all races, and every one of them was different, but they gave me a lot of memories.

My family was never very stable or solid, and I know that was the reason I had so many failed relationships. My great-grandmother told me two things once.

First, she said, "A rolling stone won't gather any moss." True statement. I never was stable, and that's why I bounced around and had three failed divorces.

I'm very sorry I had two failed relationships with my two living, grown children. See, they don't look at my side, and that's why I wrote my book. I had to get my side out. I will take it to my grave that my first wife lied to me and brainwashed my kids against me. One day, she will answer to her Maker for what she did. I don't forgive her, and I never will. Why? Because God gives us children to love, not to hurt and abuse.

I loved my kids, all of them, with all my body, soul, mind. I got my heart ripped out with the blood vessels pumping my blood out. Only a few people helped me and cared about my feelings. Everyone felt sorry for my first wife and first daughter. What about me? I carried a lot of guilt and anger about losing my daughters.

The second thing she said was, "An apple doesn't fall from the tree." She was talking about my first wife and her parents.

Family is important

She also said, "What about their teeth?" My first wife's parents were pretty backwoods of Missouri.

I told my grandmother I could take her away from her parents and everything would be fine. Well, it wasn't. She was lower white class, and our marriage only lasted five years. She was a liar, a user, and had no goals for herself.

She lied about everything, even about taking birth control. Her genes and mine didn't match, and we had one out of four chances of our children coming down with Niemann-Pick. I wish now I would have never married her. I could have saved myself a lot of pain that caused me to become a hurting man.

My family was mostly my forty-five-year-old friend, Steven Andreas. Thanks, Steve and Beth. My mom told me life starts at fifty. She didn't lie.

She also told me she was proud of me and I was the man. She asked me how I handled losing two daughters. I said I did it with God, and I had to live on for myself and my son.

I miss my parents so much. Life is short, and after my mom's death, I felt so alone. Before I never knew where she was after my parents divorced. I felt guilty. She left to find herself and lost her kids along the way. Somewhere at the end, it wasn't about her money or what she was leaving me; it was about a forgiving closure.

I love you, Mom, and can't wait until we see one another again.

My dad, "Old Jolly Roger," was a firm but fair father. Every time I go fishing, he crosses my mind. Dad was a beer drinker and a true fisherman. He loved to salt and freshwater fish. I have already outlived him, and I'm a bigger and better man.

My whole life my only wish was for him to be my dad without a beer can.

My special thanks goes out to my great-grandmother, Juanita James Shelton. She showed us all love and kept us all together as a family. She was a very good person and a strong lady.

Managing my deer lease in 2022

Well, I got a spike in November 2021. All my hunters got a deer and hogs, and we are looking toward a season in 2022. Tom, the land owner, is going to buy 250 more acres.

That means more security checks, disking, and mowing; more hunters to manage. Went and bought two four-wheelers. I plan on driving around the whole property on a four-wheeler to look for trespassers.

In Texas we take our hunting very *seriously*. We don't like poachers or trespassers.

I'd like to welcome Ricky as a new friend and member. Robert is an old security friend and a new member. One of these guys probably will kill a big buck, so big they could win a big-buck contest.

I'd like to thank Mr. Snook of Livingston. He is like a grandfather to me and gives us all a great place to hunt.

People Loving Their Pets

I remember like it was yesterday. My aunt Shelly bought a full-blooded Yorkie named Cowboy. I used to stop by my grandmother's house to visit her and Cowboy.

I fell in love with him, and when he passed away, a big part of me went with him. Shelly taught him to play dead. Donna and I bought a $500.00 full-blooded Yorkie called Hunter. He is a mess. Follows me around like my shadow. He dislikes people and all dogs. I take him with me on my security checks. From the dash, if he sees anything, he goes ape crazy.

Well, we just got back from Galveston. We bought a $500.00 small female Yorkie and named her Paris Helton. We will breed them and sell the female puppies for $800.00 and the males for $500.00.

Show me the money!

I should have been breeding a long time ago.

C H A P T E R   2 7

Living My Dreams: Attempting to Live to Be One Hundred Years Old

My family and I moved out of our home in Shepherd, Texas. So the landlord sold the trailer, and we lost a lot of money on that deal. But we were offered 10.2 acres and a two-story house, which needed some work by Mr. Snook.

Well, no one can tell the future, but I want to live to be one hundred. I love and live life to the fullest, so I feel like that's why I only sleep four hours a night. I guess, deep down, I'm afraid I'm going to miss something.

My dreams are to be peaceful and live each day like it's my last. I want to enjoy seeing my eight-year-old grow into a teenager and then a young woman.

I want to complete my property, and in ten years, when it's paid for, Donna and I will sell our double-wide and 4 acres for $250,000.00, go out and buy a new small RV, travel, and see most of the United States. After that my life will prosper and be complete.

Last thing to do is have a wonderful funeral, and my life will be over.

C H A P T E R 2 8

The Woman of My Dreams

Well, I look back on my long road dealing with the opposite sex, a woman. After dating seventy-eight different women and marrying four of them, I've decided I don't understand a woman more today than when I did at sixteen years old. When I met Miss Donna, my last wife, I knew something was different. We've been together for eight years. No major fights and we have never separated or broken up.

She is a simple woman, easygoing, sweet, with a heart as big as Texas. She and I have a lot in common. I've always have given her a hard time. Never hit her, and I promised I would never step out on her. Well, I've kept my word, and I never felt like any other woman was my soulmate. I've known couples that have divorced after thirty years. Will we make it thirty years? Who knows?

Growing Old with My Wife

Well, growing old with Donna is going to be fun.

She has six things wrong with her medically, and I have three things wrong with me.

I'd love to take care of her when she gets older. Her dad always gave his wife, Barb, what she wanted. I've done the same for Donna. The only complaint I've had with her, she is not so verbal and doesn't show her husband a lot of attention.

I've already made arrangements through Land of Memory. When we go, I hope we go close together, and I wouldn't want to live without her. Thanks for loving me and putting up with my good and bad *sides*.

I've always loved you since the first time I saw you. Love, Bad Brad.

C H A P T E R   3 0

Final Ending

Well, this is it. My wife and I bought a wooded house in Texas between Livingston, Texas, and Woodville. I bought her a Ford SUV, and all I got in return was "I hate you." Well, the month was December. As usual, I had to do all the Christmas decorations. I was exhausted. In a marriage, the couple is supposed to do things together. In my case, she would take all fifteen of her pills, watch cable, hallmark, and neglect me for five years—my daughter also suffered from both of us—and neglect herself and her sleep. When I disturbed her, she would tell her friends and family that I was bipolar and crazy, abusing her physically and mentally.

I was damned if I do and still damned if I don't.

Mental problems

Well, when my phone broke, I gave her money for herself and needed her to run to Walmart to get me a $30.00 phone. She got me a $70.00 phone, and when she got home, we snapped broke again. Yes, I did push her, and she pushed me. I grabbed her, and with both of us being sick overweight with diabetic, we fell down. My wife started screaming once I got off. Then, in ten years, another disrespect happens at her so-called best friend's double-wide located in Shepherd, Texas. Well, the law got called again, and I, an officer of twenty-five years, waited for back up. When they arrived, or should I say before I went upstairs, she brought me a card and said, "I don't want to fight, and I don't want you to divorce me." Me and Bad Brad ripped that card up, and I said, "Bullshit! I'm done."

"A big lie stretching the truth"

She hated herself, hated me, hated the house, and hated life. It broke my heart, but it is what it is as my wife's sister says.

After the Polk County Sheriff's Department and DPS arrived, my so-called wife almost went to jail for telling the officers untrue lies. I started to press charges, but I didn't.

Well, I told her to go back to her next of kin. What a joke. We loved and hated, but when she put her hands on me and she lies, the handcuffs or the camel back broke. She left a few days later, and I was so relieved. And so was Bad Brad.

She and I let our daughter visit my sister in Louisiana. I am glad.

The pushing match

My daughter wasn't home. I called my sister and told her the truth. Then I decided to sign a paper that would prevent my ex-wife from treating me like she did to other men. It was sad that I never knew she was a liar, a user, and a lot of other things. She changed to the worst. I'm not going to waste a tree on her other children and her two grandkids. It was a big joke. I was only liked by my mother-in-law. She saw the light. All the best and the rest had physical and mental problems.

I should have never married her because I did not marry her for her family. Drama, jealous moments—living and judging are not my style.

I tell the truth about people. I am saying it again, "Right is right. Wrong is wrong."

No one likes the truth but will believe a lie. How sad.

So do what's right and don't lie to me or Bad Brad. I will get you good. I fell out of love with her and the whole situation.

Now I have my inner peace. Divorce is over. You never know what you have until it's gone. I will never speak to any of them or especially another one of my exes. To "the last one," I would like to say I'm sorry. You were so sick you couldn't change to keep our family together. I was wrong also. I'm sorry we couldn't work it out.

Some called him Bad Brad. I'm not perfect, but I'm closer to getting to heaven than others. Some people need to quit blaming me for their problems. Grow up. Let it go. Now back in the uniform. Yes, I'm doing what God intended me to do. A good friend, officer, Christian, dad, and husband. Now I can concentrate on myself, my daughter, and other people who appreciate me.

My goal is my next book *The Great Outdoorsmen*. People who know how to respect wrote off my true stories. Yes, hunting, camping, fishing, and natural walks where nature makes you smile. I'm sorry. I have enjoyed writing the stories of my life.

I swear to tell the whole truth and nothing but the truth.

For the woman who said I had too many stories, I say, "Catch up if you can."

Get or make you a life as interesting as mine. Jealousy ruins a lot of relationships. For the other woman, "You need to take a bipolar pill and change and grow up. You can have her back. I'm done. I feel so lucky to be done with all of you. Go to church and listen."

For my stepsons, be thankful I was willing to help.

It is over. My heart and brain are crystal clear.

Thank you.
Mr. D. Bradley

SPECIAL THANKS

I'd like to thank the book publisher that helped me get my story out there and my book on the shelf. I enjoyed writing these chapters, and I hope someone can read my book and get something positive out of my life experiences. Life is not perfect, and it is filled with a lot of ups and downs.

Special thanks goes out to Steven, a longtime hunting friend; Donny Keys, my mentor, for believing in me; and John Allen for helping me to find myself.

My grandmother Juanita James Shelton for being my mother and great-grandmother in one.

My parents, even though they divorced when I was a little boy since my mother was out of my life for a long time and had excellent closure.

My only stepfather, Sonny. You will always be my dad in my eyes, and thanks for allowing me to hunt on your lease.

My dedicated wife, best friend, soulmate, and the only woman that really loved me and stood by me without a breakup or a divorce. We have accepted each other, and we are one.

My two daughters loved me unconditionally and never hurt me with their mouths and actions.

Prayer

Thank you, Heavenly Father, for your many blessings and delivering me from evil and giving me the strength to live for my other children, people, and myself to complete the circle of life. Amen.